ALIVE AND ACTIVE

健 “幸” ライフ志向の総合英語

Masamichi Asama

Nicholas Lambert

Iwao Yamashita

NAN'UN-DO

ALIVE AND ACTIVE

Masamichi Asama
Nicholas Lambert
Iwao Yamashita

Download Audio

音声ファイル
無料 DL
のご案内

このテキストの音声を無料で視聴（ストリーミング）・ダウンロードできます。自習用音声としてご活用ください。
以下のサイトにアクセスしてテキスト番号で検索してください。

https://nanun-do.com　テキスト番号［ **512176** ］

※ 無線 LAN（WiFi）に接続してのご利用を推奨いたします。

※ 音声ダウンロードは Zip ファイルでの提供になります。
お使いの機器によっては別途ソフトウェア（アプリケーション）の導入が必要となります。

Read by
Kyle Card
Shizuka Anderson

※ Alive and Active 音声ダウンロードページは以下の QR コードからもご利用になれます。

まえがき

超高齢社会の到来により、生産人口の減少および社会保障費の増加から、国策としての「健康寿命の延伸」が盛んに叫ばれるようになりました。しかし、人間個々にとっては、遥か昔より今日にいたるまで、元気で最後まで暮らせる、いわゆる「美しい老い」は不変の目的と言えるでしょう。そのような潜在ニーズを反映してか、多様な健康食品の販売に始まり、フィットネスクラブの乱立にいたるまで、健康ビジネス産業の盛況ぶりには目を見張るものがあります。昨今のコロナ禍にあっては、健康意識の増大はますます高まっていっているといっても過言ではありません。しかし、ステイホームをしばしば奨励されるコロナ禍では、どうしても外的刺激に触れる機会が減じ、自律的な健康志向努力にも自ずと限界がありそうです。このことは学びに関しても決して例外ではありません。無機質なオンライン授業ばかりだと、どうしても思考が停滞し、学びの意欲が削がれがちになってしまいます。

そこで本英語テキストは「思考する英語」をテーマに全体を編集いたしました。重厚な内容の本文に加え、外国語運用能力において語彙力が非常に重要な位置を占めている点をも考慮し、コンテクストを見極めながら行う語彙学習や論理的思考およびクリティカルシンキングを養う問題を散りばめました。さらには精度が高くなったウェブ翻訳ツールの影響で、「英作文」の授業を廃止した大学も出現している実際をも鑑み、英作練習問題にも工夫を凝らしてみました。

本テキストがコロナ禍で浮上し始めたワクチン接種や高齢者の生活スタイルをはじめとする問題に対して、少しでも学習者の意識が先鋭化されれば幸いです。

なお、刊行にあたり、南雲堂編集部の加藤敦氏には大変お世話になりました。ここに深く感謝の意を表します。

2022年10月1日
編著者代表　淺間正通

本テキストの特徴

Warm-up Exercise

TOEIC の最初に出題される写真・イラスト描写問題です。まずは手軽に取り組めるビジュアルな学びから入り、入門的なリスニング力を培います。

Inspiration Exercise

本文中に出現する語彙について定義したリスニング問題ですが、一部はディクテーション方式にもなっていますので、トップダウン型処理とボトムアップ型処理の併用によって答を導く問題となっています。

Word-attack Exercise

いわゆる多義語を抽出しています。あくまでも本文中に出現している語（網掛け）についての意味用法を問うものです。ここでは短文ではありますが、コンテキストを見極めながら正確なリーディングにおける判断力を養う意図から問題設定してあります。3 択となっていますが、判断基準に迷う場合には本文中の対象語の意味を繰り返し確認するようにしてみてください。

Comprehension Exercise

本文の内容に対する正確な理解を問う問題となっています。本文の全体的な文脈をしっかりと押さえながらチャレンジしてみる必要があります。

Discourse Exercise

パラグラフリーディングにおける結束性（cohesion）および一貫性（coherence）についての認識を応用した問題です。文脈重視で順序だてないとしっかりとした英文として成立しません。導く接続詞などは重要なヒントとなりますので、文法力も動員しながらチャレンジしてみてください。

Production Exercise

英作文用の練習問題ですが、多様なヴァリエーションで設定しています。特にウェブ翻訳ツールでの語用的誤用に関わる問題にあっては、翻訳ツールが和文のどの箇所に引っかかって過ちを犯したのかなど、分析的な捉え方も必要となってきます。

CONTENTS

Unit 1

Nutrition and Fitness

【栄養とフィットネスの正しい関わり合い】

We all know that we can support good physical health by eating well and getting sufficient exercise. These two components are central to the quality of life: they keep us *alive and active* (the title of this textbook). We can eat almost anything to stay alive, but with the right combination of nutrition and exercise we can also have an active and satisfying life. In this first reading we are going to examine how nutrition and fitness work together to build a healthy life.

But what exactly is a healthy life? Most people would say that it is when we look and feel good and are able to do the physical activities that we need or want to do in our daily lives. According to a lot of research, regular exercise is important to having a healthy life, but nutrition has an even greater impact. Because of this, many sport trainers and coaches consider healthy food intake (providing good nutrition) as the primary fitness goal. When we eat right, we feel healthier, stronger, more confident and ultimately happier.

Nutrition is the process by which living things receive the food necessary for them to grow and be healthy. This process doesn't mean simply to consume food or drink. It also involves the selection and consumption of food and drinks that contain important nutrients that bodies need to grow well and maintain health: water, vitamins, minerals, protein, carbohydrates, and so on. However, as our bodies pass through different developmental stages (e.g., infant to teenager, young adult to elderly) our nutritional needs change in type and quantity. That is because our body structures and physical abilities change as we grow older (e.g., body sizes increase, muscles develop in strength, mobility and control). We can help these physical changes by matching our nutrition to our physical development and needs. Moreover, through using exercises that complement our nutritional intake and are appropriate to our age, physique and general health, we can improve our overall level of fitness and well-being.

Some research studies have shown that having proper nutrition in the first year of life is the most important for lifelong health. For instance, children who are overweight at the age of one are more likely to struggle with weight problems throughout their lives than children who are at healthier weights at that age. For healthy bone growth, children have a greater need for calcium than adults do. The elderly also need more calcium than younger adults so as to strengthen bones that are weakening with aging. Thus, good nutrition can help with both physical development and maintenance, and can also aid in health improvement during times of injury or illness.

The nutritional needs for performing a physical activity depend on three main factors: intensity, duration, and type. One part of a food's nutritional value is its quantity of calories. A calorie is a measurement of the amount of energy a certain food provides to fuel physical activities. For high intensity activities such as playing football or skiing, there is a larger calorie need than for less intensive activities such as taking the dog for a walk. Doing an activity for an hour requires more calories than doing it for 30 minutes. An aerobic activity (or cardio) such as distance running uses a lot of oxygen and raises the heart rate. As a result it burns more calories than an anaerobic (or non-aerobic) activity such as sprinting or weight-lifting which is short in duration but higher in intensity.

Lifestyle choices related to physical fitness (e.g., interests and hobbies, types of employment) as well as factors such as age, gender, and general health condition produce varying nutritional needs. A common saying is that “we are what we eat.” So if we don’t make the best nutritional choices, who we are will probably not be who we should be.

Notes

l. 11 **intake** = an act of taking something into the body
l. 13 **ultimately** = finally (e.g. He thought seriously of quitting, but ultimately decided to stay on.)
l. 17 **nutrient**「栄養物」
l. 18 **carbohydrate**「炭水化物」
l. 19 **infant**「幼児期」
l. 24 **complement** = to add to something in a way that improves it
l. 25 **appropriate to...**「…に適した」
l. 25 **physique**「体格；からだつき」(e.g. He has a fine physique.)
l. 26 **well-being**「健康（な状態）」
l. 33 **thus** = in this way
l. 37 **intensity**「激しさ；強度」
l. 44 **anaerobic**「無酸素の」⇔ aerobic
l. 45 **sprint**「（特に短距離間を）全力疾走する」

Warm-up Exercise

A 次のサプリメントに関する情報を見たのち、1 – 3 の質問文と選択肢を聴いて正しい答を選びなさい。

Nutrition Facts	
Serving Size 1/4 Cup (30g)	
Servings Per Container About 38	
Amount Per Serving	
Calories 200 Calories from Fat 150	
	% Daily Value*
Total Fat 17g	**26%**
Saturated Fat 2.5g	**13%**
Trans Fat 0g	
Cholesterol 0mg	**0%**
Sodium 120mg	**5%**
Total Carbohydrate 7g	**2%**
Dietary Fiber 2g	**8%**
Sugars 1g	
Protein 5g	
Vitamin A 0%	• Vitamin C 0%
Calcium 4%	• Iron 8%
*Percent Daily Values are based on a 2,000 calorie diet.	

1. What is this label?
   (A) (B) (C)

2. What is the meaning of “Daily Value”?
   (A) (B) (C)

3. What is the “Serving Size” of this product?
   (A) (B) (C)

Inspiration Exercise

B 次の 1-3 の英文を聴いて下線部を補い、さらにその意味を表している本文中の語を答えなさい。

1. It is the noun form of the word which means "______________________________ ______________________________ as food and the way that they influence your health."

   In other words: (   )

2. It is the verb form of the word which is defined as "to use fuel, energy, or time, ______________________________."

   In other words: (   )

3. The word means ______________________________.

   In other words: (   )

Word-attack Exercise

C 次の 1-3 の本文中に出現している語と最も近い意味で使用されている英文を (A) (B) (C) の中から選びなさい。

1. examine
   - (A) The doctor who examined my throat didn't say anything about the disease.
   - (B) Each student will be examined orally by a team of teachers in order to graduate.
   - (C) Please examine the error information printed in the book.

2. involve
   - (A) It is important to involve all the group members in the discussion.
   - (B) I do not want to be involved in the new project.
   - (C) Global warming closely involves the issue of rising sea levels.

3. raise
   - (A) If you want to ask a question at the meeting, you will need to raise your hand.
   - (B) The Bank of England raised interest rates last week in order to reduce inflation.
   - (C) I was born in Tokyo but raised in Kyoto.

Comprehension Exercise

D 本文の内容に即して、次の英文の内容が正しければ T (True) を、誤っていれば F (False) を記しなさい。

( ) 1. Bones in the early phase of development necessitate more calories.
( ) 2. People with thinning bones need more calcium.
( ) 3. A long swim would require more calories.
( ) 4. Physically mature adults would require less calcium.
( ) 5. Walking slowly would need less calories than walking quickly.

Discourse Exercise

E 次の出だしに続く英文を意味の通るように並べかえなさい。

We all know that we can support good physical health by eating well and getting sufficient exercise. These two components are central to the quality of life: they keep us alive and active.

A. In order to gain that satisfaction, quality nutrition can help with the physical development of children as well as the body maintenance of the elderly.

B. The right combination of nutrition and regular exercise is essential to having an active and satisfying life.

C. Consequently it is important to make the best nutritional choices to match our varying nutritional needs.

Answers. ( ) ☞ ( ) ☞ ( )

Production Exercise

F 下記の英文の（　）内の語を並べ替えて意味の通る英文にしなさい。また、完成した英文の和訳も示しなさい。

Exercise addiction is a type of (have / behavioral / effects / that / can / addiction / negative) on physical health, mental health, and general way of life.

英文：..

....

和文：..

....

Unit 2

24 / 7 Fitness Clubs

【いつでもどこでもフィットネス】

One of the most popular ways for an adult to try to keep fit is to join a fitness club. Such a club usually offers a variety of training equipment and facilities, group training courses, personal training, advice for self-training programs, shower and sauna facilities, and private lockers for storage of personal belongings. In addition, it may provide extras such as towels, equipment or clothing rentals, sales of exercise aids and nutritional supplements, massage services, and light meal services. Fitness clubs have a range of membership fees, from single day passes to long-term contracts with rates matched to contract length: the longer the contract, the cheaper the effective daily rate. For example, a club might charge $10 for a single day pass, $60 for a week-long pass, and $200 for a monthly pass.

Many people sign a long-term membership contract, thinking that they will be motivated to come regularly to the club because they won't want to waste such a big sum of money. However, even people who are highly motivated when they join a club often stop attending regularly because they are busy, tired, injured or ill, or else find that the hard effort needed to carry out their fitness programs is simply not enjoyable. Moreover, it is common for working people to discover that the daily fitness club schedule does not allow them much time to visit after work. After all, many people have to rush to work in the morning, while after work they may need time for family or friends, meals, rest and relaxation. Traditionally, fitness clubs have had opening hours from 8–9 a.m. until 9–10 p.m. That leaves very little time for busy adults to go to a fitness club during weekdays. Although they could exercise at their clubs on the weekends, people are often busy with work or social activities on those days. Even if club members do have the time for the gym on weekends, they frequently manage only one or two visits per week or month—which is insufficient exercise for general well-being. Thus, the average club member would be better off buying single day passes than taking out a longer contract.

Many workers have evening or night jobs, so that their free time is late at night or in the early morning, and thus outside the opening hours of traditional fitness clubs. In addition, there are some people who are *early birds* or *night owls*, feeling naturally more energetic outside the normal hours of daily activity. These people may prefer to go to a fitness club late in the evening or early in the morning. Because of this problem of access, recently more and more fitness clubs worldwide have extended their opening hours to satisfy their clients' schedules and desires. Furthermore, since there is an over-abundance of fitness clubs in many cities, there is often a lot of competition to find and keep new club members. So fitness clubs that are always open (24 hours, 7 days a week) have become more common in recent years.

Initially, 24/7 fitness clubs only provided access to club facilities such as weights and exercise machines. Responding to complaints by members who wanted full use of club facilities and services (requiring service staff such as lifeguards, personal trainers, and fitness instructors) during the night hours, fitness club chains without closures such as 24/7 Fitness Club or Anytime Fitness are opening branches worldwide. In this way, they attract more club members and avoid many complaints about poor access or services. As the famous American inventor Benjamin Franklin once commented, “Well done is better than well said.” With fitness club access at any hour, members can do more than *talk* about getting exercise: they can *do* exercise at their own convenience. For that reason, visits to the gym may become more frequent and longer membership contracts more cost-effective.

Notes

l. 04 **personal belongings**「身の回り品；所持品」
l. 26 **insufficient**「不十分な；不足な」(n. insufficiency)
l. 27 **be better off...**「…の方がもっと良い状態になる」(e.g. Perhaps I was better off not knowing.)
l. 28 **taking out a longer contract**「長期契約を結ぶ」
l. 31 **early bird**「早起きの人」
l. 31 **night owl**「夜更かしする人；夜型人間」
l. 36 **over-abundance**「過剰」
l. 47 **Benjamin Franklin**「ベンジャミン・フランクリン」ベンジャミン・フランクリン (1706-1790) は，アメリカ合衆国の政治家，外交官，著述家，気象学者，発明家で，アメリカ独立宣言の起草委員の一人.
l. 47 **Well done is better than well said.**「良い言葉より良い行いの方が勝るものだ」ベンジャミン・フランクリンの名言の一つ.「どんなに良いことを言ったとしても良い行動には勝てない」という意味.

Warm-up Exercise

A 次の写真を見たのち、1-3 の質問文と選択肢を聴いて正しい答えを選びなさい。

1. How many people are jumping?
   (A) (B) (C)
2. How many pairs are facing each other?
   (A) (B) (C)
3. What is the woman in front doing?
   (A) (B) (C)

Inspiration Exercise

B 次の 1-3 の英文を聴いて下線部を補い、さらにその意味を表している本文中の語を答えなさい。

1. The word represents ______________________________,
   especially those that can be carried.
   In other words: (   )

2. This is the situation in which ______________________________.
   In other words: (   )

3. This is ______________________________ about something.
   In other words: (   )

Word-attack Exercise

C 次の 1-3 の本文中に出現している語（下記対象語が複数出現していても、ここでは本文中に網掛けしてある語）と最も近い意味で使用されている英文を (A)(B)(C) の中から選びなさい。

1. pass
   (A) I have to pass The National Museum of Modern Art on my way to the university.
   (B) Would you please pass me the salt?
   (C) I lost my boarding pass somewhere around Gate 15.

2. charge
   (A) How much do you charge for a bottle of wine made in Bordeaux?
   (B) Who will be in charge of this project while I am away for a month?
   (C) The part-time worker at the gas station didn't know how to charge up the batteries.

3. rest
   (A) My girlfriend suddenly tried to rest her head on my left shoulder.
   (B) When driving long distances, you should take a rest every two hours.
   (C) Please enjoy the rest of your stay in this hotel.

Comprehension Exercise

D 本文の内容に即して、次の英文の内容が 24/7 型のフィットネスクラブに関するものには Y (Yes) を、そうでないものには N (No) を記しなさい。

(　　) 1. Morning people and night people have difficulty in making good use of them.
(　　) 2. Using single day passes can never be more economical than paying for a long-term membership.
(　　) 3. You can take lessons from your personal trainer.
(　　) 4. Regardless of their size, they provide around-the-clock service.
(　　) 5. Fitness clubs do not allow members to use the gym on weekends.

Discourse Exercise

E 次の出だしに続く英文を意味の通るように並べかえなさい。

One of the most popular ways for an adult to try to keep fit is to join a fitness club.

A. And some fitness clubs go even further, by offering unlimited access to their facilities and services 24/7.

B. They often do this by offering opening hours to match their clients' schedules.

C. Such clubs offer a variety of facilities, equipment and training programs.

Answers. (　　　　) ☞ (　　　　) ☞ (　　　　)

Production Exercise

F 下記の英文は、無料のウェブ翻訳ツールで和文入力して訳出したものであるが、語用的誤用が生じて不自然となっている。正しく直しなさい。

【入力和文】

君はエアロバイクを速くこげばこぐほどカロリーを燃焼する。

【訳出文】

* The faster you burn an aero bike, the more calories you burn.

Ans. ……………………………………………………………………

…………………………………………………………………….

Unit 3

Exercise and Brain Function

【運動で脳年齢の若返り】

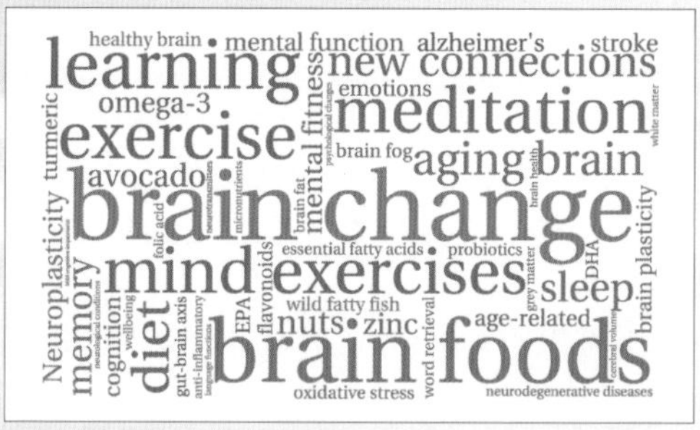

As adults become older—particularly after 40 or 50 years of age—their physical strength naturally weakens. Their bones become more brittle, their muscles tend to shrink, their body becomes less flexible than when they were younger. Recent research shows that mental abilities also tend to diminish as we get older, so it is common for reaction times to slow down. For instance, nerve signals sent to and from the brain sending a message for a driver to apply the brakes may take longer for older adults than in their youth, resulting in a delayed physical response to apply the brakes (and potentially causing traffic accidents). Moreover, memory loss generally occurs as one gets older, sometimes to the extent that a person develops a serious condition such as dementia or Alzheimer's disease.

Physical weakening is a natural result of aging, though maintaining regular physical exercise can slow down this process or even counteract it. Similarly, the knowledge that is held in memory can be preserved for longer periods of time through different mental exercises that fight against memory loss or even more severe brain problems. There is a lot of evidence that humans maintain both physical and mental skills through practice. We tend to learn new things by *doing* them; we remember how to do these things by *repeating* them. This process is sometimes called "muscle memory" and it applies both to thoughts and actions. But how does exercise influence the brain and provide support for the learning and maintenance of new information and physical and mental skills?

Being physically active has a lot of health benefits, including reducing the risk of getting heart disease, stroke, and diabetes. It can also help people to lose weight, lower blood pressure, increase muscle strength, improve flexibility, and even prevent depression. Exercise helps memory and thinking directly by reducing insulin resistance and inflammation as well as by releasing chemicals that aid in the growth of new cells and blood vessels in the brain (e.g., *brain-derived neurotrophic factor* or BDNF), and even by adding to the quantity and survival of new brain cells. Exercise also helps to improve people's sleep and mood, leading to the reduction of stress or anxiety.

The principal reason why exercise improves brain health is that it makes the heart beat faster, causing more blood to flow to the brain. Because blood is carrying oxygen, as the rate of blood flow increases more oxygen is provided to the brain—which is important since the brain uses more oxygen than any other part of the body. In effect, oxygen is the brain's "fuel," delivered by the blood. Another important benefit to physical exercise is that it can directly protect memory and thinking skills by increasing the size of the hippocampus—the part of the brain responsible for verbal memory and learning. The increase in oxygen from exercise feeds the hippocampus, which grows larger in volume and hence in capacity to learn and remember information.

The American Heart Association recommends "150 minutes per week of moderate-intensity aerobic activity or 75 minutes per week of vigorous aerobic activity, or a combination of both, preferably spread throughout the week." These exercises may include household chores such as carrying groceries, washing the floors, or even standing instead of sitting. A healthy lifestyle includes a balance of *aerobic* exercise (for elevation of heart and breathing rates) and *anaerobic* exercise (non-aerobic activity focused on muscle strengthening). However, aerobic exercise is the most important for brain function because it boosts the heart rate and consequently more oxygen goes to the brain. Long distance running, brisk walking, spinning (riding on a stationary bicycle), cross-country skiing, and even dancing are examples of aerobic exercises.

Notes

l. 02 **brittle** 「もろい；折れやすい」
l. 03 **shrink** 「縮む」
l. 04 **diminish** 「衰える；落ちる」(n. diminution)
l. 06 **apply the brakes** 「ブレーキをかける」
l. 10 **dementia** 「認知症」
l. 13 **counteract** 「対抗する；妨げる」
l. 23 **diabetes** 「糖尿病」
l. 26 **insulin** = a hormone in the body that controls the amount of sugar in the blood
l. 26 **inflammation** 「炎症；燃焼状態」
l. 27 **blood vessel** 「血管」
l. 28 **neurotrophic** 「神経栄養の」
l. 37 **hippocampus** 「海馬」
l. 40 **hence** = for this reason
l. 42 **moderate-intensity** 「中強度の」
l. 42 **vigorous** 「激しい；精力的な」
l. 44 **household chores** 「家事」(e.g. She busied herself with household chores in the morning,)
l. 49 **boost** = raise
l. 50 **brisk** 「元気のよい；きびきびした」
l. 50 **stationary bicycle** 「サイクリングマシン（固定自転車）」

Warm-up Exercise

A 下記のイラストを見たのち、1-3の質問文と選択肢を聴いて正しい答を選びなさい。

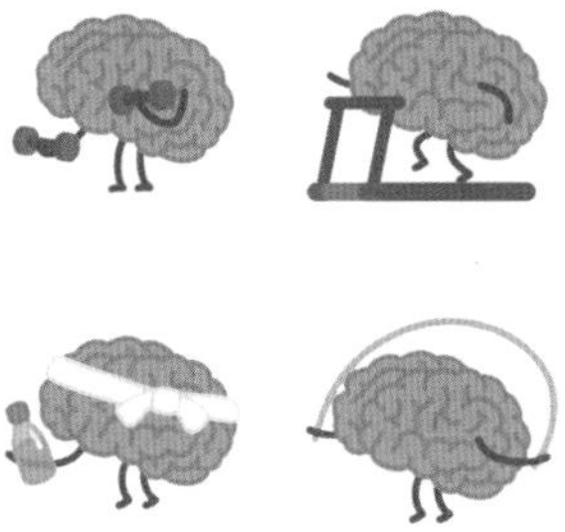

1. What do these icons stand for?
   (A) (B) (C)
2. What is the one with the headband holding?
   (A) (B) (C)
3. Which one is jumping rope?
   (A) (B) (C)

Inspiration Exercise

B 次の 1-3 の英文を聴いて下線部を補い、さらにその意味を表している本文中の語を答えなさい。

1. The word means ______________________________ information, experiences, and people.
   In other words: (   )

2. This is the body's quality of ______________________________.
   In other words: (   )

3. This is ______________________________, especially to keep your house clean.
   In other words: (   )

Word-attack Exercise

C 次の 1-3 の本文中に出現している語と最も近い意味で使用されている英文を (A)(B)(C) の中から選びなさい。

1. stroke
   (A) My grandfather is currently in hospital because he had a stroke.
   (B) In the pool I tried the most basic swimming stroke today.
   (C) How many strokes does the difficult kanji have?

2. depression
   (A) Japan has been in a deep economic depression for years.
   (B) Mrs. Watson was suffering from depression last year.
   (C) The depressions in the sand are made by scorpions.

3. deliver
   (A) The doctor has just delivered her third baby.
   (B) The morning paper has just been delivered.
   (C) The prime minister of Japan will deliver a short speech this evening.

Comprehension Exercise

D 本文の内容に即して、次の英文の内容が正しければ T (True) を、誤っていれば F (False) を記しなさい。

(　　) 1. By training our muscle memory we can keep not only physical skills but also mental skills.
(　　) 2. Taking physical exercise leads us to improve our sleeping habits.
(　　) 3. Physical exercise makes blood flow more actively and contributes to an increase in the size of the hippocampus.
(　　) 4. According to advice given by The American Heart Association, moderate aerobic activity is a key to the formation of healthy life styles.
(　　) 5. A delayed physical response in applying the brakes of a car is usually the result of muscular weakening.

Discourse Exercise

E 次の出だしに続く英文を意味の通るように並べかえなさい。

Memory loss generally occurs as one gets older.

A. For instance, certain physical activities such as moderate and intense aerobics help maintain memory.

B. People may develop serious conditions such as dementia or Alzheimer's disease.

C. However, practice helps humans maintain both mental and physical skills.

Answers. (　　　　) ☞ (　　　　) ☞ (　　　　)

Production Exercise

F 次の和文に対する英訳が完成するように（　　）内に適する語を入れなさい。

65 歳未満で発症したアルツハイマー病は、若年発症型アルツハイマー病とみなされる。

Alzheimer's disease is considered to be younger-onset Alzheimer's (　　　　) it affects a person before (　　　　) (　　　　) (　　　　) 65.

Unit 4

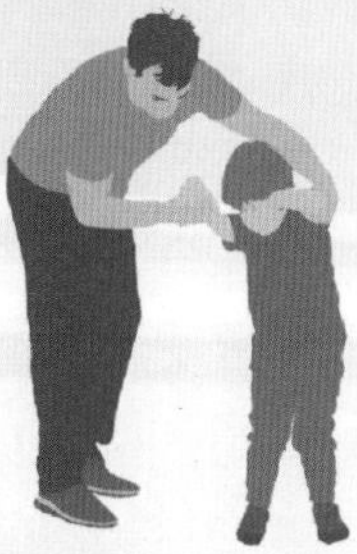

Exercise Therapy

【運動療法は質と TPO 次第】

Injuries and illnesses, whether serious or minor, happen to everyone. No matter how you try to protect yourself, you are bound to get sick or hurt accidentally—especially if you participate in sport activities. Sometimes recovery from such a problem requires very little treatment: cleaning and bandaging a cut, resting, or taking a painkiller and so on. However, for many health problems the treatment and recovery processes are more complex, take a longer period of time, and may involve a lot of pain. Aside from these occasional health troubles, some people suffer from chronic or permanent health conditions that require specialized care. For example, people may suffer disabilities caused by incurable diseases like multiple sclerosis (MS). In these cases, it is common for therapeutic exercise (exercise therapy) to be included as part of the treatment and recovery program. This type of exercise may also be used for the prevention and maintenance of both physical and mental health.

Most people are aware of the benefits of physical exercise to our body's fitness. In addition, there are many mental health gains from such exercise. For one thing, chemicals that improve your mood are released as a result of doing physical exercise, in particular endorphins and serotonin (often called the "happy hormone"). Some of these chemicals stimulate the parts of your brain that are responsible for memory and learning. You also tend to feel less stress, feel more confident, and have a better sense of your own self-worth if you keep up a regular exercise program: you look better and feel better about yourself.

The precise types of exercises used in therapeutic programs depends on your personal needs. The importance of therapeutic exercise when dealing with injuries, illnesses or disabilities has already been mentioned. Another type of exercise therapy is intended for young children who need to develop their muscle coordination or improve their physical abilities. Furthermore, mothers may need exercise therapy to recover from pregnancy and delivery. Other exercise therapies help people to learn to use assistive devices like splints or braces, or to maintain balance in order to avoid falls.

The design of a plan for exercise therapy should take into account your individual needs, goals, age, and current level of fitness. A poorly designed exercise program can destroy your motivation and ability to follow it. Moreover, when you have an injury or are in chronic pain, exercise may be quite difficult or painful. If you try to do exercises that don't match your health condition, you might even make your problem worse. So it is vital to consult with a qualified and experienced exercise specialist before you attempt to recover on your own. After all, exercise therapy can be quite complex, since each type of exercise relates to its own specific muscles or parts of the body. Moreover, individual exercises are usually very competitive and hence can easily be overused. The duration of each exercise, the number of *reps* (repetitions) to be performed, and the intensity (speed and amount of effort and energy required) needs to be adjusted as you gradually improve your health. An exercise specialist is likely to be very knowledgeable about program design and implementation and therefore should be consulted before you start any new exercise system. It is also a good idea to review your fitness goals and exercise plans with a doctor—to make sure that the therapy suggested is approved medically.

A good physical therapist creates a care plan that is a detailed guide for your therapy. Sometimes therapists provide hands-on assistance during these exercises, such as having you push your feet against their hands for muscle strength training. (For this kind of performance, you should expect the therapist to ask for your permission before touching you.) The therapist may also be a teacher, showing you how to do special exercises for better mobility, muscle strength, or flexibility. Through the verbal encouragement and careful monitoring of your progress that you receive from your exercise therapist, you can distinguish a good therapist from a poor one. And, if you are lucky, the therapist may become a good friend!

Notes

l. 02 **be bound to**「～するにちがいない」
l. 08 **chronic**「慢性の」
l. 10 **incurable**「（病気が）不治の；治療不能の」⇔ curable
l. 10 **multiple sclerosis (MS)**「多発性硬化症」神経細胞を覆う部分に傷ができることで起こる脳と脊髄の障害．神経機能の低下を伴い，日本では特定疾患に認定されている指定難病である．
l. 17 **endorphins**「幸福ホルモン」脳内で機能する神経伝達物質の一つで，多幸感をもたらすと考えられている．
l. 17 **serotonin**「セロトニン」アミノ酸のトリプトファンから作られる有機化合物で，脳内，血清，胃粘膜に多く分布し，神経伝達やけがをした組織の血管収縮などの働きをする．
l. 18 **stimulate**「刺激する；興奮させる」
l. 27 **pregnancy**「妊娠；妊娠期間」(e.g. She appears to be in her sixth or seventh week of pregnancy.)
l. 28 **splint**「（骨折の）添え木；副木」
l. 28 **brace**「（体の一部を固定する）装具」
l. 30 **take into account...**「…を考慮に入れる；…を考慮する」
l. 43 **implementation**「実施；実行」

Warm-up Exercise

12

A 次の写真を見たのち、1-3 の質問文と選択肢を聴いて正しい答えを選びなさい。

1. What is the man wearing on his thighs?
   (A)　(B)　(C)
2. What is the woman in the picture doing?
   (A)　(B)　(C)
3. What exercise is the man working on?
   (A)　(B)　(C)

Inspiration Exercise

13

B 次の 1-3 の英文を聴いて下線部を補い、さらにその意味を表している本文中の語を答えなさい。

1. This is a kind of medicine ______________________ our pain.
   In other words: (   )

2. This is ______________________ that makes it difficult for someone to use a part of their body properly.
   In other words: (   )

3. This is what we call a person who is skilled in ______________________ for physical or mental health.
   In other words: (   )

Word-attack Exercise

C 次の 1-3 の本文中に出現している語（下記対象語が複数回出現していても、ここでは本文中に網掛けしてある語）と最も近い意味で使用されている英文を (A)(B)(C) の中から選びなさい。

1. condition
   (A) Please do not forget to read the terms and conditions of this product.
   (B) There are three conditions necessary for looking after dogs successfully.
   (C) Getting moderate exercise every day keeps your mind and body in good condition.

2. fall
   (A) Please take care not to fall on a slippery floor.
   (B) Enough rain to flood the field will fall in mid-summer.
   (C) Study hard, or you will fall behind in class.

3. vital
   (A) Exercise keeps a person young and vital.
   (B) The vital signs of the patient are stable for the moment.
   (C) It is often said that perseverance is vital to success.

Comprehension Exercise

D 本文の内容に即して、次の英文の内容が正しければ T (True) を、誤っていれば F (False) を記しなさい。

(   ) 1. You need more serious treatment for injury than for other health problems.

( ) 2. If you are more engaged in doing physical exercise, more hormones that make you happier are produced.

( ) 3. The more problematic your injury and your health condition are, the more you must depend on an experienced physical therapist.

( ) 4. It is also vital for a family doctor to be well-aware of the duration, the number of repetitions and intensity of each exercise.

( ) 5. A good therapist behaves like a teacher who gives instruction on the special exercises, gives appropriate verbal encouragement and conducts careful monitoring.

Discourse Exercise

E 次の出だしに続く英文を意味の通るように並べかえなさい。

Aside from other occasional health troubles, some people suffer from chronic or permanent health conditions that require specialized care—for example, people with disabilities caused by incurable diseases like multiple sclerosis (MS).

A. So good therapists create a care plan and provide hands-on assistance.

B. To deal with these problems, therapeutic exercise may be used as part of the treatment and recovery program as well as the prevention and maintenance of both physical and mental health.

C. Moreover, keeping up a regular exercise program can bring a number of mental health gains.

Answers. ( ) ☞ ( ) ☞ ( )

Production Exercise

F 本文で記されている内容に即して、次の英文に対する理由を英語で答なさい。

Why is serotonin often called “the happy hormone”?

Ans. ....

....

Unit 5

To Age or Not To Age

【高齢化社会を支える新たなテクノロジー】

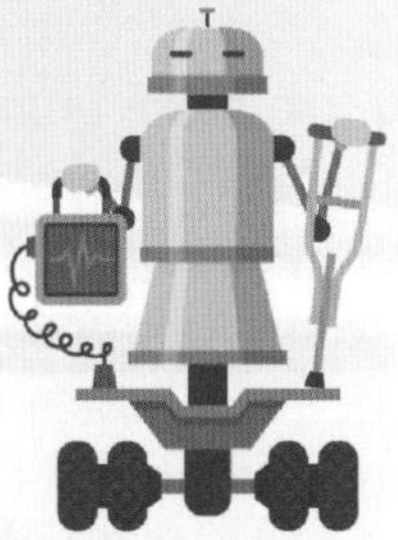

Most older adults want to live independently and actively in their own homes as long as they can. Living at home and being able to carry out daily activities such as gardening, cooking, or shopping, gives people a sense of satisfaction, pride and enjoyment of life. However, the physical, mental, and social effects of aging tend to increase our needs for outside help as we get older. Our bodies gradually lose their physical strength, flexibility, mobility, beauty, and ability to deal with disease or injury. In turn, our increasing physical limitations can frustrate us and lead to feelings of depression and anxiety. Moreover, due to restrictions in mobility, retirement from working life, or the deaths of friends, the opportunities to meet other people are often reduced with aging and thus leading to feelings of social isolation and loneliness. Without sufficient social contact there can also be negative effects on mental health: hastening the loss of mental skills, leading to forgetfulness or even mental disorders like dementia or Alzheimer's.

These issues are of great concern due to the rapidly aging world we live in. As the elderly population increases as a percentage of any society, the needs for adequate support services for the elderly will continue to expand. Yet because of social changes like falling birth rates, smaller families, greater mobility, and higher numbers of females in the workforce, there are fewer family members available to care for the elderly than in the past. Consequently, more dependence is placed on public or private support services, causing rising costs for care workers, facilities, and equipment. Indeed, demand for these resources is greater than availability, particularly in poorer countries.

As a result, a new industry called *gerontechnology* has developed through a merging of the two fields of gerontology and technology. Gerontology is the scientific study of the biological, psychological and sociological aspects of aging; technology here is the research and design of equipment to solve practical problems of the elderly. The idea is that technical developments will aid the elderly to stay in their own homes (often called *living in place*) as long as possible and with less need for home care workers, thus delaying a move into an assisted living home.

Let's look at a real-life situation. My 96-year-old mother is still living in place despite having mobility restrictions. In her home she has a *mobile chair* mounted on rails and powered by electricity for movement between floors in her house. She also has a foldable *walker* with wheels for movement support and shelves for carrying food trays or books from room to room. Furthermore, she wears a *remote care watch* which activates a signal to a private care service whenever she has a fall. Like many elderly, my mother also has increasing hearing loss and uses hearing aids during conversations. But her hearing aids often need battery changes which are hard to manage because of the small battery size. Therefore, my mother also has a tablet computer for communication whenever her hearing aids aren't functioning well. For telephone conversations, she may soon get a captioned telephone allowing her to type and receive messages on a screen instead of talking and listening.

Gerontechnology is an exciting and rapidly evolving field. Robotics and other IT devices as well as improvements in home architectural design are making living in place easier for older adults. The active aging industry includes safety, health and remote care, and fitness and wellness technologies. Smart-home technology such as voice-activated lighting, air conditioning, and even cooking makes household management simpler for everyone who can afford it. As driverless cars become more common in future, frail elderly may be able to go shopping on their own. Already there are robot pets to provide companionship without the need for feeding or walking, as well as robots which can converse after assessing the moods and interests of their elderly owners. These tools designed to reduce social isolation and loneliness are growing in popularity and sophistication. As can be seen, there is a great future and employment opportunities in gerontechnology!

Notes

l. 11 **social isolation**「社会的孤立」
l. 13 **mental disorder**「精神疾患」
l. 19 **in the workforce**「働いて」
l. 24 **gerontechnology**「ジェロンテクノロジー」ジェロントロジー (gerontology) とテクロノロジー (technology) を組み合わせた造語で，老化に関する科学と近代技術の融合領域.
l. 25 **merge** = unite
l. 35 **foldable**「折り畳める」
l. 39 **hearing aids**「補聴器」
l. 43 **a captioned telephone** = a special telephone that has a built-in screen to display each conversation in text (captions) during the call
l. 45 **evolve**「進展する」
l. 51 **frail** = weak
l. 54 **assess**「判断する」

Warm-up Exercise

A 下記のイラストを見たのち、1-3 の質問文と選択肢を聴いて正しい答を選びなさい。

1. Where does the man feel pain?
   (A) (B) (C)
2. What kind of pain does the woman have?
   (A) (B) (C)
3. Where is the man when he starts to feel the pain?
   (A) (B) (C)

Inspiration Exercise

16

B 次の 1-3 の英文を聴いて下線部を補い、さらにその意味を表している本文中の語を答えなさい。

1. This word means “________.”
   In other words: (　　　　　　　　　　)

2. This word means “________.”
   In other words: (　　　　　　　　　　)

3. This word means “________
   and the problems of elderly people.”
   In other words: (　　　　　　　　　　)

Word-attack Exercise

C 次の 1-3 の本文中に出現している語と最も近い意味で使用されている英文を (A) (B) (C) の中から選びなさい。

1. issue
   (A) Have you read the latest issue of the journal?
   (B) Two politicians exchanged their opinions on the controversial issues.
   (C) When is your driver’s license going to be issued?

2. demand
   (A) There is a great demand for nurses in Ukraine right now.
   (B) You should demand that he gives you back the money soon.
   (C) I demand to speak to a manager.

3. afford
   (A) The window affords a beautiful view out over the city.
   (B) Jane doesn’t feel she can afford any more time away from work.
   (C) My father can only afford to buy a K-car at the moment.

Comprehension Exercise

D 本文の内容に即して、次の英文の内容が正しければ T (True) を、誤っていれば F (False) を記しなさい。

(　　) 1. Long-term immobility can lead to the feeling of loneliness and depression.

(　　) 2. The elderly have more opportunities to meet other people, which have a positive effect on their mental health.

( ) 3. People living now can benefit more from the rising industry of gerontechnology than those in the past.

( ) 4. The population proportion of elderly people is rapidly decreasing in the modern world.

( ) 5. Many supportive devices such as mobility chairs, foldable walkers, and remote care watches enable elderly people to live in place.

Discourse Exercise

E 次の出だしに続く英文を意味の通るように並べかえなさい。

The physical, mental, and social effects of aging tend to increase our needs for outside help as we get older.

A. Yet the social challenges such as falling birth rates, smaller families, and greater mobility result in fewer family members being available for elderly care.

B. This active aging industry includes safety, health and remote care, and fitness and wellness technologies.

C. Therefore, an exciting and rapidly growing field called gerontology is helping to replace family support.

Answers. (　　　) ☞ (　　　) ☞ (　　　)

Production Exercise

F 下記の英文の（　　）内の語を並べ替えて意味の通る英文にしなさい。また、完成した英文の和訳も示しなさい。

Many experts say that communication robots (more / elderly / help / independent / be / people) in their everyday lives.

英文：………………………………………………………………

……………………………………………………………….

和文：………………………………………………………………

……………………………………………………………….

Unit 6

Riding into the Future

【高まる電動自転車人気】

Cycling is one of the most environmentally-friendly means of transportation and is a great way to get exercise. Modern bicycles have many types: road, touring, BMX(Bicycle Motocross), hybrid (city), standard, and so on. However, normal bicycles can present problems for some people. Carrying heavy loads or transporting small children can make balancing or pedaling difficult, especially when cycling uphill or on rough road surfaces. As people grow older, they may even find cycling without a heavy load challenging because of problems with balance and lowered muscle strength.

To deal with these issues, an electric bicycle (e-bike) industry has been rapidly developing. First invented in the late 19th century, the modern electric bicycle has a dynamo which changes energy of movement into electrical energy, and is one of two types: power-assist (also called pedal-assist) which can be switched on to assist the cyclist's power while pedaling; *full-power* which can replace pedaling entirely so the rider can take a rest. Riders have a range of power boost settings from *eco* (low) to *turbo* (high), depending on how much assistance to pedaling the rider wants.

Full-power e-bikes are used mainly by elderly people and courier services, whereas power-assist types are currently the most common in use because they are cheaper and give the cyclist more exercise. Regardless of type, however, the main effects are that many cyclists can travel longer distances, carry bigger loads, and get exercise without getting so tired. As a result, e-bikes are practical for daily life transportation—for shopping, courier services, transporting young children, commuting to work, and so on.

Nevertheless, there are some drawbacks to current electric bicycles. Adding a motor and a battery pack to a bicycle frame makes the e-bike much heavier than standard bicycles. This can be a problem for someone who wants to carry an electric bicycle on a trip by car. The weight of the e-bike makes it much more difficult to lift onto a bicycle rack attached to a car. Furthermore, if the e-bike falls over it is harder to raise it up again off the ground. Also, the battery requires regular recharging: the batteries for cheaper e-bikes are often heavier and need to be recharged more frequently than the lithium batteries on more expensive models. In addition, the power of an e-bike can cause a cyclist to travel at a dangerous speed, so the motor may automatically shut off when the speed reaches a maximum speed of 30-50 kph (depending on the model). Moreover, e-bikes are pricy: a decent e-bike will set you back at least 150,000 yen; a top-quality e-bike may cost as much as a motorcycle.

Despite these issues, the advantages of electric bicycles have meant that they are growing dramatically in popularity, particularly in Europe and China. Between 2016 and 2017 e-bike sales worldwide increased by more than 90%. In the Netherlands, for example, there were more e-bikes sold in 2018 than traditional bicycles. In China, there are estimated to be at least 120 million e-bikes in use. In North America, both Uber and Lyft are setting up e-bike rental services, while the Ford car company is testing an e-bike sharing service in San Francisco.

More and more people in large cities are finding e-bikes to be practical for getting through congested traffic, so they can fulfil their urban transportation needs more quickly and cheaply than by car, and without causing air pollution. Maintaining exercise by cycling for longer in one's life than in the past is possible because of the e-bike. Moreover, e-bikes now come in the same types as traditional bicycles—available in fat, cargo, commuter, recreational, mountain, and racing bike styles. This variety enhances their appeal to cyclists. Bicycle manufacturers are working to reduce the weight of the batteries and frames, and are even studying the application of solar energy for battery charging. New designs are likely to make e-bikes even more prevalent and useful as time goes on.

Notes

l. 11 **dynamo**「発電機」
l. 17 **courier service**「宅急便」
l. 24 **drawback**「欠点」
l. 35 **pricy**「高価な」
l. 35 **decent**「まともな；そこそこの」
l. 35 **set ~ back...**「~に…の費用がかかる」
l. 42 **Uber**「ウーバー」米国サンフランシスコに拠点を置く配車サービス企業で，世界中の市場で事業を展開している.
l. 42 **Lyft**「リフト」米国サンフランシスコに拠点を置く配車サービス企業で，世界最大の配車市場である北米に注力した事業を展開している.
l. 51 **enhance**「高める；増す」(e.g. The gorgeous dress enhanced her beauty.)
l. 54 **prevalent** = in general use ; common

Warm-up Exercise

A 下記の写真を見たのち、1-3 の質問文と選択肢を聴いて正しい答えを選びなさい。

1. Where are they cycling?
   (A) (B) (C)
2. What are they riding?
   (A) (B) (C)
3. How would you describe the people in the picture?
   (A) (B) (C)

Inspiration Exercise

19

B 次の 1-3 の英文を聴いて下線部を補い、さらにその意味を表している本文中の語を答えなさい。

1. This is the system in which ______________________________,
   aircraft, or ships.
   In other words: (   )

2. The word means “something coming from ______________________.”
   In other words: (   )

3. This is the outside or ______________________________.
   In other words: (   )

Word-attack Exercise

C 次の 1-3 の本文中に出現している語と最も近い意味で使用されている英文を (A) (B) (C) の中から選びなさい。

1. present
   (A) My parents gave me a present for my birthday.
   (B) We should pay more attention to the present state of affairs.
   (C) Mr. Yamada will present his idea to the board at next month’s meeting.

2. common
   (A) Because Mary and Pascal did not speak a common language, they couldn’t talk to each other.
   (B) Since he had a heavy cold, he didn’t visit the House of Commons.
   (C) It is common for teenagers to sleep more than 9 hours.

3. application
   (A) If you are interested in the Japan Festival, please fill in this application form.
   (B) The young engineer learned the practical application of the theory he had studied in the classroom.
   (C) I don’t know how to uninstall this application software in my computer.

Comprehension Exercise

D 本文の内容に即して、次の英文の内容が正しければ T (True) を、誤っていれば F (False) を記しなさい。

(   ) 1. Elderly people may find it difficult to cycle even without a heavy load.

(　　) 2. The e-bike of a power-assist type can fully replace pedaling.
(　　) 3. One disadvantage of an e-bike is that its heavy weight can cause lifting problems.
(　　) 4. Though e-bikes are gaining popularity in Asia, that trend is not happening in Europe.
(　　) 5. Bicycle manufacturers are trying to develop new types of e-bikes that are lighter than earlier models.

Discourse Exercise

E 次の出だしに続く英文を意味の通るように並べかえなさい。

Modern bicycles have many types: road, touring, BMX, hybrid (city), standard, and so on; yet, since even standard bicycles can still present problems for some people, e-bicycles have been developed.

A. Regardless of that issue, the popularity of e-bikes is still growing rapidly all around the world.

B. Nevertheless, an e-bike frame tends to be much heavier than those of standard bicycles due to the addition of a motor and a battery pack.

C. The benefits of e-bicycles include travelling longer distances, carrying bigger loads, and getting exercise without feeling exhausted.

Answers. (　　　　) ☞ (　　　　) ☞ (　　　　)

Production Exercise

F 下記の英文は、無料のウェブ翻訳ツールで和文入力して英訳したものであるが、和文の解釈において語用的誤用が生じている。正しく直しなさい。

【入力和文】

この電動自転車の電池をもたせるにはどうすればよいのですか？

【訳出文】

* How can I get the battery of this electric bicycle?

Ans. ....

....

Unit 7

3D Printing for Healthcare and Sport

【健康スポーツへの画期的技術応用】

When you were a child, did you ever draw a picture of a futuristic-looking object like a spaceship or a flying car? Can you imagine how much more interesting it would have looked to you if you could have drawn it in three dimensions (3D)? Well, now you can! A technology called *3D printing* is now being used in many industries for designs, models, prototypes, and products. But what is 3D printing and how does it work?

Essentially, 3D printing (also called *additive manufacturing*) is a method of creating solid objects in three dimensions from a digital file. In normal manufacturing an object is made by cutting it out and shaping it from metal, plastic, or other materials. On the other hand, 3D printing involves adding layers of material gradually on top of each other until the object is created. In this process, far less material is needed to produce a solid object than in traditional manufacturing.

It is a little hard to explain this technology, but let's attempt to do so in simple terms. To start this process, you need to create a 3D model using IT tools such as a 3D scanner or modelling software. However, if a model already exists for the object you want to make, you can download it from a 3D archive instead. After you have your 3D model, the next step is to use slicing software which slices your model into many horizontal layers. The resulting digital file is then used in a special 3D printer which prints the object layer by layer.

3D printing uses many types of technologies and materials for manufacturing in a wide variety of commercial industries. For instance, in the field of health care, 3D printing is commonly applied to the production of surgical tools, medical implants and prosthetics (artificial devices attached to the human body internally or externally) as well as dental products like tooth implants and crowns. In future it is likely that many artificial organs for the human body will be created using 3D printing technology. Similarly, 3D printing is becoming central to the design and production of sport equipment aimed at improvements in sport performance, injury management, adaptive sport (for persons with physical disability), and so on.

In medicine one of the biggest challenges for 3D printing is the production of artificial materials that mimic (behave in a similar fashion to) the behavior of natural human tissues. Generally it has been easier to develop more rigid materials for procedures like hip replacements than it has been to create softer tissue replacements (e.g., for artificial hearts). Furthermore, more research is needed on the fatigue of 3D printed objects so as to predict the duration time before an artificial object wears out and requires replacement.

In competitive sport, one of the current problems facing sport authorities is that athletes can have unfair advantages in equipment if they use 3D printing for improved performance that competitors do not have access to. Elite athletes with rich sponsorship may be able to afford deals with 3D printing manufacturers that poorer athletes cannot obtain. As an example, after Eliud Kipchoge became the first athlete to run a marathon in under two hours in 2019 using a new Nike shoe design that the other runners had no access to, his shoe type was banned from future competitions in order to maintain equality.

On the other hand, for high tech yacht races like the America's Cup, 3D printing for developing radical and innovative yacht designs is considered perfectly acceptable. In preparation for the 2019 Formula 1 car racing season, Ferrari used 3D printing to make a new kind of paint that gave their racing cars better aerodynamics and less weight than the models of other race car manufacturers.

Whether in health care, sport or any other manufacturing industry, 3D printing allows 100% customized products to be built quickly and precisely for individual needs. It has also increased the speed for the research, design, and mass production of the materials and tools for these industries. Hence, the future of 3D printing looks very bright!

Notes

l. 01 **futuristic-looking**「未来風の」
l. 17 **additive manufacturing**「付加製造技術」
l. 19 **horizontal**「水平の」⇔ vertical
l. 24 **implant**「移植片」
l. 24 **prosthetic**「補綴；人工」
l. 24 **artificial organ**「人工臓器」
l. 32 **mimic** = copy closely ; imitate
l. 33 **tissue**「組織」
l. 33 **rigid**「堅くて曲がらない」
l. 37 **wear out**「すり減る」
l. 42 **Eliud Kipchoge**「エリウド・キプチョゲ」ケニアのマラソン選手．2019年10月12日にウィーンで行われた特別レースで，1時間59分40秒というタイムをマークした．
l. 50 **aerodynamics**「空気力学；航空力学」
l. 53 **precisely**「精密に；正確に」

Warm-up Exercise

A 下記の写真を見たのち、1-3の質問文と選択肢を聴いて正しい答えを選びなさい。

1. Where are they?
   (A) (B) (C)
2. What are these men doing?
   (A) (B) (C)
3. What are these men wearing?
   (A) (B) (C)

Inspiration Exercise

B 次の 1-3 の英文を聴いて下線部を補い、さらにその意味を表している本文中の語を答えなさい。

1. This is a measurement of something, like ____ ________________________, diameter, etc.
   In other words: (   )

2. This is financial support ____, usually given by groups or companies.
   In other words: (   )

3. This is something that is used ____.
   In other words: (   )

Word-attack Exercise

C 次の 1-3 の本文中に出現している語（下記対象語が複数出現していても、ここでは本文中に網掛けしてある語）と最も近い意味で使用されている英文を (A)(B)(C) の中から選びなさい。

1. solid
   (A) The dining table used by our family is made of solid oak.
   (B) I always wear a solid color cap when I go out.
   (C) There is no solid evidence that lack of sleep causes depression.

2. crown
   (A) A dental crown is used to rebuild and safeguard the top of a tooth which has been damaged.
   (B) The king wears a crown when he inherits the throne.
   (C) Fortunately, we had the chance to meet the crown princess of Denmark.

3. object
   (A) We can frequently use pronouns for both direct and indirect objects.
   (B) One of my friends said, "I saw a strange flying object last night."
   (C) The taxi driver strongly objected to the new parking rules in his city.

Comprehension Exercise

D 本文の内容に即して、次の英文の内容が 3D プリントに関するものには Y (Yes) を、そうでないものには N (No) を記しなさい。

(　　) 1. An object is made by cutting it and shaping it from raw materials.
(　　) 2. A product consists of multiple layers added gradually on top of each other.
(　　) 3. The manufacturing process needs far more material to produce a solid object compared to other type of production.
(　　) 4. Many artificial organs for the human body will be produced by this technology in the future.
(　　) 5. The technology must overcome the problem of durability of the products.

Discourse Exercise

E 次の出だしに続く英文を意味の通るように並べかえなさい。

Three dimensional printing is now being used in many industries for designs, models, prototypes, and products.

A. But one drawback of 3D printing is that it can sometimes lead to improved athletic performance which give athletes unfair advantages.

B. As an example, the file process is used in the production of surgical tools, medical implants, and prosthetics.

C. Basically, it is a method for creating solid objects in three dimensions from a digital file.

Answers. (　　　　) ☞ (　　　　) ☞ (　　　　)

Production Exercise

F 次の和文に対する英訳が完成するように (　　) 内に適する語を入れなさい。

3D プリントでつくった家に関して言えば、私の父より詳しい者は誰もいない。

When it (　　　　) (　　　　) 3D printed houses, (　　　　) (　　　　) (　　　　) more than my father.

Unit 8

Adaptive Sports

【不可能を可能にするスポーツの進化形】

Many people enjoy playing or watching sports. Sport may be viewed as entertainment, recreation, exercise, education, character building, skill training, injury prevention or rehabilitation, or a career. Thus, there are many possible motivations for engaging in or observing sporting events. Participation may be within a range from active to passive, varying by age, gender, fitness level, physical or mental abilities, and interests. There are also different ways to categorize sports: competitive vs. non-competitive, individual vs. team, professional vs. amateur, indoor vs. outdoor, local vs. universal, and so on. Ultimately, for anyone who has any interest in sport there are nearly always opportunities to participate in some way in their local area. However, that has not always been true in the past.

Until the 20th century, in many societies sport was considered primarily or even exclusively a male domain. Even to this day, professional male athletes and teams have tended to receive much higher salaries and more media exposure than female players. In some societies women have not even been permitted to be spectators of sport in public places until very recently. Similarly, in the past there have been limits or even bans on sport participation based on race, sexual orientation, religion, or for other reasons. Moreover, historically people with physical or intellectual disabilities have had little chance to be actively involved in sport (except as circus-like performers for the entertainment of people without disabilities).

Fortunately, times have changed and the majority of the world recognizes that all people—regardless of gender, sexual orientation, race, or ability—have the same rights, basic needs, and motivations, including those related to sport. To accommodate people with various physical or intellectual disabilities, *adaptive sport* (sometimes called *para-sport* or *disability sport*) has become available globally. For people with physical disability, there are adaptive sport programs at local community centers or sport clubs which take into account their special physical needs. Some of these programs can eventually lead to athletic participation in international competitions such as the Paralympics. Similarly, the Special Olympic organization includes many adaptive sports for people with intellectual disabilities.

Because there are physical or mental limitations for people with disability, in order for them to participate in many sports, the rules, equipment, or facilities often need to be altered in some way. When changes are made to an existing sport for people with disability (e.g., wheelchair basketball) the sport is called an *adapted* sport. In adapted sports the playing area may be smaller, the equipment may be redesigned in special ways, rules may be simplified, or playing times may be altered. On the other hand, some sports cannot be adapted at all. Instead, new sports have been invented for use by people with specific disabilities—such as *torball*, a team sport for the visually impaired using a ball containing bells inside.

Still other sport programs are aimed at promoting *inclusivity*: encouraging people without disabilities to share a sport with those who have a disability. The Special Olympics has a section called *Unified Sports* in which each team is composed of players with and without intellectual disabilities competing together. This helps to build friendship, understanding, and skill among all participants.

As a side issue somewhat unrelated to adaptive sport itself, at the elite level of sport there has also been some movement towards inclusivity. For example, some athletes with a physical disability have been allowed to compete at the Olympics. The earliest of such athletes was the gymnast George Eyser who won three gold, one silver, and one bronze medal at the 1904 Olympics while wearing a wooden leg. However, some sport experts believe that with advances in medical technologies people with disabilities using implants or prosthetic limbs may soon have unfair advantages by being able to compete with greater strength, speed or flexibility than those without these assistive aids.

Regardless of such controversies, it is clear that adaptive sport has come of age, as it gains in popularity, availability, and public support. Sport should be a pastime for anyone who is interested in it, and we are lucky to live in a world where that is becoming increasingly possible.

Notes

l. 05 **vary by**「～によって異なる」
l. 13 **domain**「領域；分野」
l. 25 **accommodate**「～に対応する」
l. 35 **alter**「変える；変更する」（adj. alterable）
l. 41 **torball**「トーボール」目隠しをしてボールを転がし，相手チームのゴールに入れてその得点を競う視覚障害者の球技.
l. 52 **gymnast**「体操選手」
l. 52 **George Eyser**「ジョージ・エイゼル」米国の体操選手．1904 年のセントルイス大会に木製の義足で出場し，たくさんのメダルを獲得した.
l. 55 **prosthetic limb**「義肢（義足・義手）」
l. 58 **controversy**「論争；議論」

Warm-up Exercise

24

A 下記の写真を見たのち、1-3 の質問文と選択肢を聴いて正しい答えを選びなさい。

1. What are they using to race?
   (A)　(B)　(C)
2. Where are they competing?
   (A)　(B)　(C)
3. What does the man in front have on his lap?
   (A)　(B)　(C)

Inspiration Exercise

B 次の 1-3 の英文を聴いて下線部を補い、さらにその意味を表している本文中の語を答えなさい。

1. This word means "________________________________."
   In other words: (   )

2. ________________________________ you want to do something.
   In other words: (   )

3. These are the people ________________________________.
   In other words: (   )

Word-attack Exercise

C 次の 1-3 の本文中に出現している語（下記対象語が複数出現していても、ここでは本文中に網掛けしてある語）と最も近い意味で使用されている英文を (A)(B)(C) の中から選びなさい。

1. observe
   (A) No one observed anything about that issue.
   (B) When a public holiday falls on a weekend, it is usually observed the following Monday.
   (C) The tourists from Japan observed wild animals at Kruger National Park in South Africa.

2. orientation
   (A) This week is the orientation period for all the freshman students.
   (B) Everyone is allowed to attend the meeting, regardless of their political or religious orientation.
   (C) How can I change the orientation of the monitor on my laptop computer?

3. intellectual
   (A) This picture book helps to promote the intellectual development of children.
   (B) Have you ever met someone who is an intellectual?
   (C) The restaurant is a popular meeting spot for intellectuals.

Comprehension Exercise

D 本文の内容に即して、次の英文の内容が正しければ T (True) を、誤っていれば F (False) を記しなさい。

(　　) 1. Until the end of the 19th century women were never allowed to participate in sport events.

(　　) 2. Para-sports are mainly practiced by people with physical handicaps.

(　　) 3. All sports can be adapted so that people with disabilities can participate in them.

(　　) 4. The idea of unified sports is to make it possible for people with intellectual problems to play with physically handicapped people.

(　　) 5. According to some observers, it is possible that physically disabled people will outperform ordinary competitors with the aid of advanced medical technologies.

Discourse Exercise

E 次の出だしに続く英文を意味の通るように並べかえなさい。

There are many possible motivations for engaging in or observing sporting events.

A. In the past, participation in sport events was limited or even banned on the basis of race, sexual orientation, religion, or other reasons.

B. As a consequence, adaptive sports are gaining popularity, availability, and public support.

C. By contrast, nowadays the majority of the world recognizes that all people should be treated equally regardless of gender, sexual orientation, race, or ability.

Answers. (　　　　) ☞ (　　　　) ☞ (　　　　)

Production Exercise

F 本文で記されている adaptive sports について、その定義となるよう出だしに続く英語を補いなさい。

Adaptive sports are sports for all people, ...

....

Unit 9

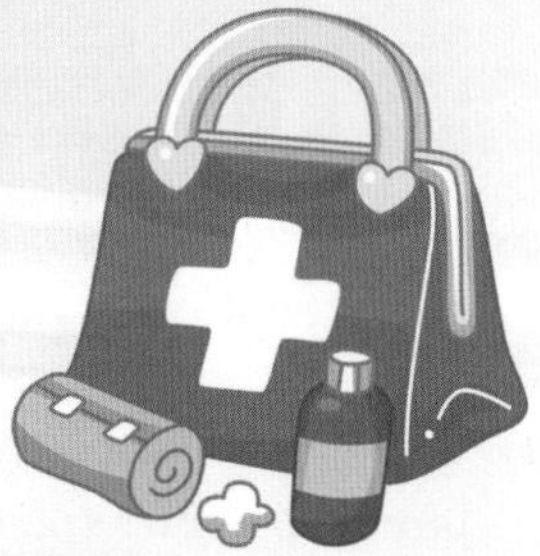

First Response
(First Aid Injury Management)

【不測の事態に備えた応急手当】

The chaos and panic that occurred within Japan right after the huge earthquake and tsunami in 2011 and throughout the world during the coronavirus pandemic commencing in late 2019 have been immense. Emergency plans and responses were inadequate, resulting in unnecessary losses of life and livelihood. There were shortages of relief staff, supplies, and emergency facilities, breakdowns in transportation systems, and poorly designed disaster plans at the governmental level and workplaces. Hopefully, lessons have been learned so that future disaster management will be more effective. Though individuals can only prepare for major catastrophes by small actions such as maintaining first aid kits and emergency supplies at home, they can also learn how to help with the medical emergencies that come with many natural or manmade disasters.

One way to do that is to take an accredited Emergency First Response (EFR, also called First Aid) training course. First Response refers to the medical steps needed to help someone in the first few minutes after a person has been injured or has suffered an acute attack of illness such as a stroke. In the time it takes for the EMS (Emergency Medical Services) paramedics to arrive after calling emergency services, the victim's medical condition may worsen without getting any help from the people around them. After all, it is a really stressful and heartbreaking experience for bystanders to watch helplessly while someone suffers or even passes away right in front of them. Through EFR training, a person can recognize and try to relieve the pain, life-threatening symptoms, and anxieties of a victim—potentially saving a life.

There are several different types of EFR certificates, but for ordinary citizens the most important courses teach the techniques of Primary Care or Cardiopulmonary Resuscitation (CPR) and Secondary Care (First Aid). Primary Care refers to the initial steps and techniques needed for dealing with life-threatening emergencies: heart or breathing problems, spinal injuries, excessive bleeding, or shock. By contrast, Secondary Care is used when the medical problem is not life-threatening or when EMS help is delayed or unavailable. A Secondary Care course teaches the first aid techniques for assessing common injuries, reducing pain, and protecting the victim from further harm. It also gives a trainee some practice in bandaging and splinting procedures.

Many countries require by law that workplaces have at least one qualified EFR worker on site at all times, so there are special courses that focus on EFR at work. Participants in sports with above-normal injury risk such as scuba diving can also get specialized EFR training related to their sport. For instance, the scuba diving organization PADI (Professional Association of Diving Instructors) requires Red Cross EFR certification in order to obtain its Rescue Diver license. Since EFR procedures are sometimes revised or else forgotten, it is a good idea to take an EFR *refresher* course every two or three years in order to keep up-to-date and be ready to assist in future medical emergencies.

The importance of CPR should not be underestimated. According to the American Heart Association, more than 90% of people who experience out-of-hospital cardiac arrest (heart failure) die every year. Moreover, cardiac arrest is the most common cause of death worldwide with well over 135 million deaths from heart failure annually. Yet if CPR is applied immediately, the mortality rate from out-of-hospital cardiac arrest can be reduced by a half or even two-thirds. Because of the danger that cardiac arrest presents, it is now a requirement in many areas for there to be an AED (automated external defibrillator) in every workplace, public facility and apartment building. This device is used to help those experiencing sudden cardiac arrest by analyzing the heart rhythm and if necessary applying an electric shock (a process called defibrillation) in order to help the heart beat properly once again.

Whether you want to be able to help a family member, a stranger, or even yourself when alone, having First Response knowledge is an asset. Since a medical emergency can occur to anyone at any time, the best time to learn EFR is right now!

Notes

l. 01 **chaos**「大混乱」(e.g. The city was in chaos after the earthquake.)
l. 03 **commence** = begin ; start
l. 03 **immense** 「非常に大きな；計り知れない」
l. 09 **catastrophe**「(多数の生命が失われる) 大惨事；大災害」
l. 13 **accredited**「認定された；公認の」
l. 17 **paramedic**「医療補助員」
l. 20 **bystander** = a person who stands near or looks on but does not take part in anything
l. 26 **cardiopulmonary resuscitation**「心肺機能蘇生」
l. 28 **spinal**「脊柱（脊髄）の」
l. 33 **splint**「(折れた骨などを) 添え木で固定する（支える）」
l. 41 **refresher course**「再教育講座」
l. 45 **cardiac arrest**「心肺停止；心不全」
l. 48 **mortality rate**「死亡率」
l. 51 **defibrillator**「除細動器」

Warm-up Exercise

A 下記の写真を見たのち、1-3 の質問文と選択肢を聴いて正しい答えを選びなさい。

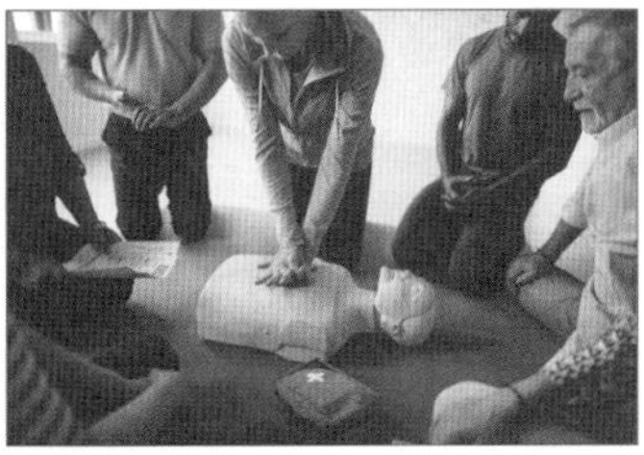

1. What is the man doing with his hands?
   (A) (B) (C)
2. How are the observers surrounding the man?
   (A) (B) (C)
3. What are they practicing on?
   (A) (B) (C)

Inspiration Exercise

B 次の 1-3 の英文を聴いて下線部を補い、さらにその意味を表している本文中の語を答えなさい。

1. This is a state of ______________________________.
   In other words: (   )

2. This is a disease that ______________________________.
   In other words: (   )

3. This is a big and terrible event which ______________________________
   ______________________ and many deaths.
   In other words: (   )

Word-attack Exercise

C 次の 1-3 の本文中に出現している語（下記対象語が複数出現していても、ここでは本文中に網掛けしてある語）と最も近い意味で使用されている英文を (A)(B)(C) の中から選びなさい。

1. occur
   (A) A bright idea occurred to me when I woke up this morning.
   (B) No one knows what could occur as a result of this event.
   (C) It is said that 20,000 species of butterflies occur in the world.

2. relief
   (A) The air conditioner in the room provided relief from the terribly hot weather outdoors.
   (B) The 5 female figures are carved in high relief on the ceiling of the central hall.
   (C) No relief pitchers were available in the bottom of the 7th inning.

3. acute
   (A) She was carried to the hospital suffering from acute appendicitis.
   (B) Sharks have a particularly acute sense of smell.
   (C) Dogs have an acute sense of hearing.

Comprehension Exercise

D 本文の内容に即して、次の英文の内容が心肺蘇生に関するものなら Y (Yes) を、そうでないものには N (No) を記しなさい。

(　　) 1. EFR care should be given right after a life-threatening accident happens.
(　　) 2. Primary Care is given in the case where patients are suffering non-life-threatening symptoms.
(　　) 3. If care is given immediately, the number of deaths caused by out-of-hospital cardiac arrest can be decreased.
(　　) 4. EFR Care is only performed where there is no access to EMS.
(　　) 5. AEDs are placed in many public places in case of a sudden heart attack.

Discourse Exercise

E 次の出だしに続く英文を意味の通るように並べかえなさい。

Hopefully, lessons have been learned so that future disaster management will be more effective.

A. EFR training can help a person relieve the pain, life-threatening symptoms, and anxieties of a victim—potentially saving a life.

B. Still, EFR refresher courses may be needed for trainees to keep up-to-date and be ready to assist others in future medical emergencies.

C. In the end, a proper knowledge of First Response is considered an asset due to the unpredictability of a medical emergency.

Answers. (　　　　) ☞ (　　　　) ☞ (　　　　)

Production Exercise

F 下記の英文の（　　）内の語を並べ替えて意味の通る英文にしなさい。また、完成した英文の和訳も示しなさい。

Knowing the basics of first aid can (in / feel / help / an emergency / prepared / you / more).

英文：..

....

和文：..

....

Unit 10

Vaccinations — Crucial or Dangerous?

【ワクチン接種をめぐる賛否両論】

In the past decade or so there has been a growing resistance to the use of vaccines that has come to be called the "Anti-Vaccination Movement." People who support this trend may be opposed to vaccination as a general health precaution. They may believe that a vaccination can actually increase the risk of catching a disease. Alternatively, they may think that the vaccination risks serious health side effects that are potentially worse than the disease itself. There are even some people with religious beliefs that reject vaccination on moral grounds. Then, there are some arguments that widespread use of vaccination in a particular society is simply too costly, so vaccinations should not be paid for by the government.

However, major health authorities such as the World Health Organization (WHO) have stated the effect of this anti-vaccination movement has been to increase dramatically the spread of the diseases for which the vaccinations had been developed. For example, many Filipino parents have been frightened away from vaccinating their children due to online reports (since proven inaccurate) that children had died due to getting measles vaccinations. The Washington Post reported in February 2019 that "doctors in the Philippine capital are battling an acute measles crisis, with more than 4,000 cases and 70 deaths so far, that has been blamed in part on an unwillingness to immunize babies after a scare surrounding a separate vaccination program last year." In 2018 the number of measles cases rose by more than 500% in the Philippines. A similar result has occurred in parts of the USA, especially in the state of Washington where the anti-vaccination movement is strong.

Though the Internet provides a lot of useful health information, much of it comes from shared blogs often with no medical or scientific support. While online searches can help people who live far from medical support services such as clinics or hospitals, too much trust can be given to online sites that are providing unproven, false or exaggerated health information, often with human interest anecdotes that can influence people emotionally into making poor health judgements.

Though vaccinations can vary in their effectiveness, most medical scientists and health organizations believe their benefits are much greater than their potential risks. For instance, the recent Salzburg Statement on Vaccine Acceptance, approved by 60 leaders in public health from the Americas, Europe, Asia, Africa, and Australia, claims that "vaccines have prevented hundreds of millions of infectious diseases—such as polio, measles, hepatitis B, and meningitis—and save up to three million lives a year." According to the WHO, the number of measles deaths worldwide dropped by 79% between 2000 and 2015 due to measles immunization.

Wherever you live, obtaining an annual influenza vaccination is highly recommended, particularly for the elderly. Even when there is little risk from certain infectious diseases in your home region, obtaining appropriate vaccinations before travelling overseas is very important, especially in tropical countries where the heat, humidity, and mosquitoes provide an ideal environment for the spread of infectious disease. Moreover, since many countries do not have the health or financial resources to provide their own citizens with the most effective vaccination programs, infectious diseases may be much more common in the regions that tourists are visiting than at home. In 2019, in addition to the USA and the Philippines, there have been outbreaks of measles in Italy, Germany, Belgium, Philippines, Guinea, Romania and Indonesia. Furthermore, hepatitis A is found throughout the world. So preventative vaccinations both for general health and travel purposes are in fact crucial. Anti-vaxxers, wake up and pay attention to reputable medical research!

Notes

l. 02 **vaccination**「ワクチン接種；予防接種」
l. 03 **precaution**「予防策；予防措置」
l. 05 **alternatively**「あるいは」
l. 14 **frighten away from ...**「脅して…から遠ざける」
l. 15 **inaccurate**「不正確な；誤りのある」
l. 16 **measles**「はしか」
l. 19 **immunize**「（ワクチンを接種して人に）免疫を与える；免疫力をつける」
l. 29 **anecdote**「逸話；秘話」（e.g. He told anecdotes about his movie work.）
l. 31 **vary in ...**「…の点で異なる；…の点で一様ではない」
l. 36 **polio**「小児麻痺」
l. 36 **hepatitis B**「**B** 型肝炎」
l. 37 **meningitis**「髄膜炎」
l. 49 **outbreak**「突然の発生；大流行」
l. 52 **anti-vaxxer**「ワクチン反対派」比較的新しい用語で，vaccine を短くした語の人称化．

Warm-up Exercise

30

A 下記の写真を見たのち、1-3 の質問文と選択肢を聴いて正しい答えを選びなさい。

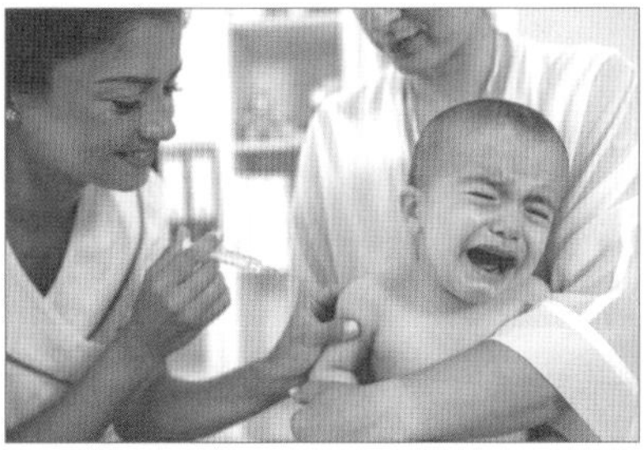

1. What is the person on the left doing?
   (A)　(B)　(C)
2. Who does the person on the left seem to be?
   (A)　(B)　(C)
3. How does the baby appear to feel?
   (A)　(B)　(C)

Inspiration Exercise

B 次の 1-3 の英文を聴いて下線部を補い、さらにその意味を表している本文中の語を答えなさい。

1. This is an action done __________ from happening.
   In other words: (   )

2. This is a power or organization having political or __________ __________.
   In other words: (   )

3. This is a short, personal story of __________.
   In other words: (   )

Word-attack Exercise

C 次の 1-3 の本文中に出現している語（下記対象語が複数出現していても、ここでは本文中に網掛けしてある語）と最も近い意味で使用されている英文を (A)(B)(C) の中から選びなさい。

1. argument
   (A) There have been a lot of arguments about who was responsible for the trouble.
   (B) I could hear my elder sisters having an argument upstairs.
   (C) Jim got into an argument with his friend at the pub.

2. case
   (A) After the concert, she put her violin back in its case.
   (B) None of us knew there was a similar case in the past.
   (C) There is a strong case for cancelling the project.

3. claim
   (A) I am going to claim proper compensation for my labor.
   (B) The teacher pointed out that the problems of SNS claim our attention.
   (C) A lot of experts claim that global warming will seriously threaten our way of life.

Comprehension Exercise

D 本文の内容に即して、次の英文の内容が正しければ T (True) を、誤っていれば F (False) を記しなさい。

(　　) 1. Some people may say that the adverse effects of vaccination outweigh the positive effects.

(　　) 2. All people opposed to vaccination think it has too many side effects.
(　　) 3. As many as 70 Filipino infant lives were saved by vaccination during measles outbreaks in 2019.
(　　) 4. Many people tend to rely too much on information online that provokes emotion.
(　　) 5. You should obtain influenza vaccinations regardless of your nationality.

Discourse Exercise

E 次の出だしに続く英文を意味の通るように並べかえなさい。

Though the Internet provides a lot of useful health information, much of it comes from shared blogs often with no medical or scientific support.

A. The correct judgement is that preventative vaccinations are important for both general health and travel purposes.

B. Too much trust on the information available on the internet could lead to making wrong judgments about health.

C. To illustrate this, the anti-vaccination movement promoted on social media is blamed for the spread of measles in the Philippines.

Answers. (　　　) ☞ (　　　) ☞ (　　　)

Production Exercise

F 下記の英文は、無料のウェブ翻訳ツールで和文入力して英訳したものであるが、和文の解釈において語用的誤用が生じている。正しく直しなさい。

【入力和文】

4 回目のコロナワクチン接種予約が明日からオンラインで可能となります。

【訳出文】

* The fourth coronavirus vaccination appointment will be available online from tomorrow.

Ans. You will be able to make a reservation ....

....

Unit 11

Medical Tourism: For Better or for Worse

【メディカルツーリズムの是非】

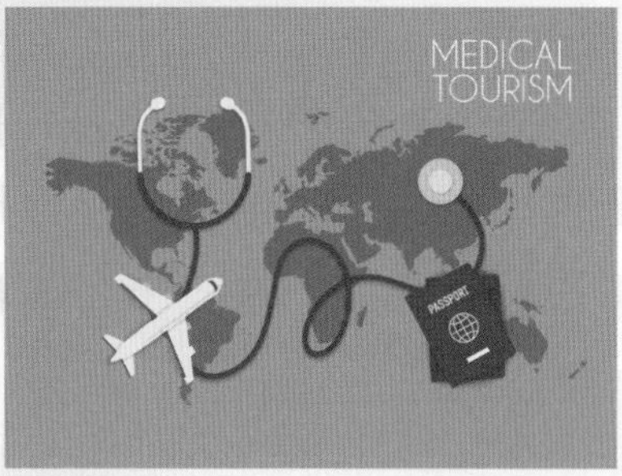

Suppose you live in a place that has limited or poor quality health services and suddenly you get a very serious illness or have a bad accident. If you are rich enough or have good health insurance protection, you can be transported to a distant hospital where the health care is much better. However, if you don't have the financial resources to pay for that, you have to accept treatment in your local area, despite its limitations. In poorer countries this is the normal situation for everyone except the wealthy—and it is one reason for low life expectancies among developing nations.

The situation is normally different for people in richer countries. Local health services tend to be much better there than in developing nations (though they may be expensive). To improve general health, many people can afford to spend time at fitness and wellness centers that provide services like exercise, yoga, special diets, massages, beauty treatments, and so on. Aside from these services, due to the ease and relatively cheap cost of international travel there is now a health industry termed "medical tourism" which is gaining ground worldwide.

Essentially, medical tourism is when a person travels across an international border in order to receive some kind of medical treatment. This is usually because treatment costs are much lower elsewhere or else a treatment unavailable at home is obtainable overseas. Although many people have public or private health insurance, some health services may not be covered under their insurance programs; moreover, the quality of their local health care may vary a lot. By travelling overseas for treatment, it is possible to go to a private hospital or clinic with specialized medicine, internationally accredited medical staff, equipment, and facilities with hospitality and accommodation that resemble a luxury resort more than a typical hospital. Often an all-inclusive package can be arranged with return transportation, accommodation and meals, medical assessment and treatment, and post-hospital care. And sometimes medical travel will be combined with optional tours or holiday stays before or after medical treatment, at a total price less than the same medical treatment alone would have cost in one's home country.

Some developing countries have well-trained health workers who are frequently hired on overseas employment contracts that give them much better salaries than in their home countries. However, the loss of such health specialists from the countries that trained them has created a brain drain in which many of a nation's best medical staff are working overseas instead of serving their fellow citizens at home. In order to reverse this trend and to take economic advantage of medical tourism, many countries have created specialized health services and facilities at affordable prices to attract patients from overseas.

One model hospital famous for medical tourism is Bumrungrad International

Hospital in Bangkok. With over 1,300 internationally-certified medical doctors and almost 5,000 support staff, this hospital is recognized as a topnotch medical facility. There are over 70 subspecialties, so this hospital has treated more than one million patients from 190 countries. In addition to its treatment work, Bumrungrad conducts cutting-edge medical research using state-of-the-art technology (such as in medical robotics). Almost every doctor can speak English, but there are also interpreters available in over 200 languages. Furthermore, there is a “medication tourism” program for patients who want to obtain drugs for their existing medical problems that are cheaper or safer than those they can get in their home countries.

Though medical tourism has many benefits for the individual patient, there are potential risks to overseas medical treatment. Some hospitals may not have the quality of service and care that is expected due to poor staff training, unsanitary or poorly-equipped facilities, lack of after-care following the patient’s return to their home country, or risky medical procedures. There is also the chance of blood clots when flying home after certain surgeries. So it is important to review the conditions carefully online and attempt to find firsthand reports from previous patients before choosing overseas medical treatment.

Notes

l. 07 **life expectancy**「平均寿命」
l. 24 **resemble**「〜のようである」
l. 34 **brain drain**「頭脳流出；有能な人材が外国に移ること」⇔ brain gain
l. 40 **Bumrungrad International Hospital**「バムルンラード・インターナショナル病院」東南アジア最大規模のメディカルツーリズムの代表的病院で，年間 120 万人以上の患者（うち **4** 割が外国人）を受け入れる．
l. 42 **topnotch**「（品質・能力などが）最高の」
l. 43 **subspecialty**「副専門分野」
l. 45 **cutting-edge**「最先端の（を行く）；最新鋭の；最前線の」
l. 45 **state-of-the-art**「最新式の；最高水準の」
l. 46 **medical robotics**「医療ロボット工学」
l. 54 **unsanitary**「不衛生な」
l. 56 **blood clot**「血栓」
l. 57 **firsthand report**「実地報告；体験的報告」

Warm-up Exercise

33

A 下記の写真を見たのち、1-3 の質問文と選択肢を聴いて正しい答えを選びなさい。

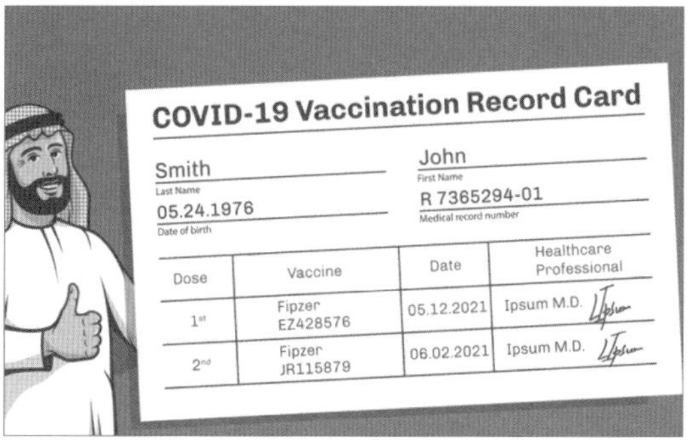

1. Where is the person depicted in the illustration probably from?
(A) (B) (C)

2. How many times has he received a vaccination for Covid-19?
(A) (B) (C)

3. What month was he born in?
(A) (B) (C)

Inspiration Exercise

34

B 次の 1-3 の英文を聴いて下線部を補い、さらにその意味を表している本文中の語を答えなさい。

1. This is the ________________________________ of guests, friends, and strangers.
   In other words: (   )

2. The word means ________________________________
   of something or someone.
   In other words: (   )

3. The word means a person ________________________________.
   In other words: (   )

Word-attack Exercise

C 次次の (1) ～ (3) の本文中に出現している語と最も近い意味で使用されている英文を (A)(B)(C) の中から選びなさい。

1. term
   (A) At this college we have important exams at the end of the summer term.
   (B) “Cutting-edge” is defined as a term synonymous with “most advanced.”
   (C) You should carefully read the terms and conditions as they were clearly stated in the contract.

2. resort
   (A) Economic sanctions will be used only as the last resort to stop the war.
   (B) Some high schools have decided to resort to recruiting English teachers from overseas.
   (C) On the island, there are lots of beach resorts suitable for holiday-makers from abroad.

3. conduct
   (A) The foreign minister conducted a series of negotiations with the French Government in a positive manner.
   (B) The guide conducted a group of travelers around the ruins of the ancient city.
   (C) The new theater was opened with a performance of the City Philharmonic Orchestra conducted by Simon.

Comprehension Exercise

D 本文の内容に即して、次の英文の内容が正しければ T (True) を、誤っていれば F (False) を記しなさい。

(　　) 1. The average life expectancy is lower in poorer countries than in richer countries.
(　　) 2. Because medical treatment overseas often costs much more than at home, many people choose to get advanced medical treatment in foreign countries.
(　　) 3. An all-inclusive package is very useful but it costs more than the same medical treatment you can get at home.
(　　) 4. In order to prevent brain drain, many countries have made their specialized health services less expensive so that foreign people can more easily get the services.
(　　) 5. In Bumrungrad International Hospital in Bangkok, almost all the staff can speak English.

Discourse Exercise

E 次の出だしに続く英文を意味の通るように並べかえなさい。

People with enough wealth or good health insurance protection have the privilege to be transported to a distant hospital where they can get better health care.

A. Despite its benefits, medical tourism can have risks such as poor staff training or lack of sanitation in poorly equipped facilities.

B. Medical tourism refers to this idea of traveling across an international border to receive medical treatment.

C. Because developed nations tend to have better local health care services than developing nations, these hospitals might even be overseas.

Answers. (　　　　) ☞ (　　　　) ☞ (　　　　)

Production Exercise

F 次の和文に対する英訳が完成するように (　　) 内に適する語を入れなさい。

自国の医療水準は決して高くないので、私はドイツで心臓手術を受けることに決めました。

Medical standards in my country are not high, so I (　　　　) (　　　　) (　　　　) (　　　　) (　　　　) in Germany.

Unit 12

Athletic Performance Enhancement

【スポーツにおける薬物使用の功罪】

Anyone who has been involved in a sport or exercise program should be familiar with the need for warm-ups before the main activity and similar cool-downs afterwards. Warm-up exercises loosen up the muscles and increase the heart rate to improve performance and help to avoid injury. Cool-down exercises help to relax the muscles once again and slow down the heart rate gradually—again helping to avoid injury and to speed up muscle recovery following intense exercise. Many athletes also use sport massage for these purposes, especially during rehabilitation to reduce muscle pain, manage soft tissue injuries (e.g., sprains and strains), or speed up recovery from more serious sport injuries like torn ligaments or bone fractures.

Massage and exercise form part of performance enhancement—a process of techniques and aids that are designed to improve the athlete's muscular and aerobic strength, speed, and endurance. There are also confidence-building and motivational mental exercises that an athlete can engage in, often in consultation with sport coaches, personal trainers or physiotherapists. These procedures can be supported by balanced and sport-appropriate dietary plans, selecting food, drinks, and supplements that provide the vitamins, minerals, and hormones needed for maximum athletic power in controlled quantities at the optimum timing for performance benefit.

There is a wide range of ongoing research (and argument) into sport diets, ranging from high carbohydrate or high protein diets for anaerobic sports like wrestling or weightlifting, to a diet with plenty of complex carbs from fruit, vegetables, grains and legumes for aerobic sports like running or soccer. Of course, in every sport the most important performance need is to get adequate hydration by drinking lots of water, sometimes supplemented by glucose for extra energy.

Because sport is competitive and often involves significant finances, professional athletes sometimes use drugs or hormone supplements to boost performance level or speed up recovery from illness or sport injury. Not every drug or hormone taken as a substance improves athletic performance, so it is legal to take some of them—especially if they are prescribed by a doctor for needed medical treatment. However, many supplements are dangerous to long-term health and may also give an athlete an unfair performance advantage over others not taking the same supplement. So sport leagues and associations maintain and continue to update lists of banned substances. Athletes, especially at the elite level, often take mandatory doping tests to check for illegal substances in their blood or urine. If athletes fail a doping test, they may face automatic suspension from their sport or even a lifetime ban for a more serious or repeated offence.

One common method of illegal performance enhancement is blood doping. In this procedure, athletes increase the number of red blood cells in their bloodstream in order to carry more oxygen from the lungs to the muscles. In that way, athletes can improve their aerobic capacity and endurance, so blood doping has become common in sports like cycling and speed skating. To produce more blood cells, an athlete can use an illegal drug, get an extra dose of blood (via a transfusion), or inject a blood substitute. There are several health risks associated with blood doping: increased chance of heart and lung diseases due to blocked arteries and raised cholesterol levels, liver damage, and possible blood infections. Therefore, almost every type of blood doping is illegal in sport.

Aside from blood doping, drugs like steroids and human growth hormones are strictly banned in sport for various health reasons. For instance, a steroid taken to improve muscle size and strength can cause permanent male infertility, denying the athlete the chance to have future children. However, in combination with good nutrition and training plans, there are ergogenic (performance) aids such as the consumption of caffeine and antioxidants or taking ice baths after exercise that can legally enhance one's athletic performance. So, an athlete doesn't need to risk punishment and potential health damage by cheating. Obeying the rules of the sport is safer and fairer to all athletes.

Notes

l. 09 **sprain**「捻挫」
l. 09 **strain**「(使い過ぎによって) 体の一部を痛めること」
l. 10 **torn ligament**「靱帯損傷」
l. 10 **bone fracture**「骨折」
l. 19 **optimum**「最適な」
l. 21 **carbohydrate**「炭水化物」
l. 22 **carbs**「炭水化物含有量の多い食べ物」
l. 23 **legumes**「豆類」
l. 25 **hydration**「水分補給」
l. 25 **glucose**「ブドウ糖」
l. 36 **urine**「尿」
l. 44 **dose** = the amount of medicine to be taken at one time
l. 45 **transfusion**「輸血」
l. 51 **male infertility**「男性不妊」
l. 53 **ergogenic**「(薬物・栄養素などが) 心身の機能を高める」
l. 54 **antioxidant**「抗酸化物質；酸化防止剤」(e.g. Fruits and vegetables abound in antioxidants.)
l. 56 **cheat**「(自己の利益のために) 不正を働く」

Warm-up Exercise

36

A 下記の写真を見たのち、1-3 の質問文と選択肢を聴いて正しい答えを選びなさい。

1. What can you see in the glass bowl?
   (A)　(B)　(C)
2. What is the woman doing?
   (A)　(B)　(C)
3. What is she drinking from?
   (A)　(B)　(C)

Inspiration Exercise

37

B 次の 1-3 の英文を聴いて下線部を補い、さらにその意味を表している本文中の語を答えなさい。

1. This word means a damage to a part of your body, ____________________

   ____________________.

   In other words: (　　　　　　　　　　)

2. This is the ability to continue doing something difficult or ____________________

   ____________________.

   In other words: (　　　　　　　　　　)

3. This is ____________________ to be taken at one time.

   In other words: (　　　　　　　　　　)

Word-attack Exercise

C 次の (1) ～ (3) の本文中に出現している語（下記対象語が複数出現していても、ここでは本文中に網掛けしてある語）と最も近い意味で使用されている英文を (A)(B)(C) の中から選びなさい。

1. performance
   - (A) The performance of *King Lear* will begin at 7.00 pm at the Globe Theatre in London.
   - (B) This race car provides its drivers with outstanding environmental and safety performance.
   - (C) He carefully goes through the whole performance of checking the oil and water even when he is in a hurry.

2. suspension
   - (A) Clifton Suspension Bridge, which was designed by William Henry Barlow, is one of Bristol's most famous structures.
   - (B) He received a one-week suspension from school for his violent and indecent behavior toward his classmates.
   - (C) The new model is equipped with computer-controlled suspension.

3. produce
   - (A) She worked as a chief director to produce a TV drama series about war-displaced orphans in China.
   - (B) Ichiro Suzuki is the greatest baseball player that Japan has produced so far.
   - (C) Our company has decided to produce high-quality kitchenware for export to north European countries.

Comprehension Exercise

D 本文の内容に即して、次の英文の内容が合法とされているものには L (Legal) を、非合法とされているものには I (Illegal) をそれぞれ記しなさい。

(　　) 1. Athletes try to avoid and recover from injuries by using sport massage.
(　　) 2. Athletes follow high carbohydrate dietary plans in order to maximize their performance.
(　　) 3. Athletes take drugs and supplements which are not subject to their sport organization's ban.
(　　) 4. To improve their endurance, athletes sometimes get a blood transfusion before their competition.
(　　) 5. Athletes take ice baths after exercise to enhance their performance.

Discourse Exercise

E 次の出だしに続く英文を意味の通るように並べかえなさい。

Sport massage can help reduce muscle pain, manage soft tissue injuries, and speed up recovery.

A. In addition, ergogenic aids combined with good nutrition and effective training plans can enhance athletic performance.

B. To support these two useful types of performance practices, adequate hydration and the intake of appropriate supplements are essential to performing sports.

C. On the other hand, caution with athletic drug use is vital, because some drugs are illegal due to their long-term health risks and the creation of unfair competition between athletes.

Answers.（　　　　）☞（　　　　）☞（　　　　）

Production Exercise

F 下記の英文の（　　）内の語を並べ替えて意味の通る英文にしなさい。また、完成した英文の和訳も示しなさい。

Doping testing is usually done in the major athletic events to find (of / traces / performance-enhancing / any / drugs) in blood or urine.

英文：...

和文：...

Unit 13

Athletic Footwear Design

【進化するスポーツシューズの機能性】

There are many types of sport footwear: jogging shoes, cross trainers, cleats (shoes with spikes on their soles for better outdoor traction or grip), basketball shoes, ski boots, diving booties—the list goes on. The materials used in their manufacture depend on their intended function and market. To select materials suitable for a specific type of sport or physical activity, manufacturers must consider many design issues such as weight, flexibility, strength, wear (endurance), cushioning and support (of sole, arch, toe and heel), closure (laces vs. alternatives like Velcro), absorption (e.g., dirt or water resistance), and appearance.

All materials used have three main features: stability, elasticity, and density. ‘Stability’ refers to how well a material maintains its shape and size as time passes. Some materials such as wood will twist or loosen when there is high humidity. Many plastics and metals will stretch or bend permanently after repeated pressure. ‘Elasticity’ is the ability of a material to bend and flex under the pressure of a force but afterwards to regain its normal shape and size. ‘Density’ is the *mass* (amount of matter) contained with a specific volume of the material—in simple terms, how large and tightly spaced each molecule of the material is. All three factors influence the shoe manufacturer’s choice of material for a particular shoe design.

In many ways the sole of a shoe is its most important feature, because this is the material that comes in direct contact with the ground. An athletic shoe needs to have a flexible sole with a suitable tread (pattern of ridges or grooves on the bottom of the sole) for the specific shoe function, as well as the ability to absorb impact. The sole receives the force or impact of a person’s foot when they run, jump, shift sideways, or come to a stop. An athletic shoe is required to have a flexible sole, suitable tread and the ability to absorb impact.

The intensity of such motions depends on factors like body weight and speed and direction of motion, so the shoe sole needs to have sufficient strength and flexibility. Because of this, a large quantity of research and development has gone into sole materials in recent times. Beyond the traditional rubber that used to be the main sole material, foam, silicon, air and gel have been added to create better cushioning in modern running shoes. A plastic called “Ethylene-Vinyl Acetate (EVA)” has changed the construction of sport shoes. Made up of tiny air bubbles that provide cushioning and absorb shock, EVA material is injected and molded into shapes which support the heels.

Shoe design also has to consider three basic running styles, labelled as *neutral*, *pronation*, and *supination*. For a ‘neutral’ running style, the foot moves forward in a straight line after the heel hits the ground. With a ‘pronation’ style, the foot rolls sideways inwards after the heel makes contact with the ground. The ‘supination’ style is the reverse, with the foot rolling outwards after ground contact. Athletes with pronation or supination may need to wear shoes that support the sides of their feet to reduce their sideways foot rolling and help their shoes to maintain natural stability. Otherwise, their shoes may wear out unevenly, resulting in loss of comfort and a shorter lifespan for the shoe.

These days, many athletes wear exercise monitoring devices on their wrists or ankles to measure the effects of exercises while simultaneously performing them by counting steps, distances, the amount of calories burned, blood pressure, and so on. The footwear company Puma has improved on this idea with its RS-Computer sneaker by installing a miniature computer monitor inside the sole of the shoe. The sport footwear industry is highly competitive, so there are very high financial rewards for innovative designs like Puma's. In 1970 there were only 5 basic sneaker models in the USA, whereas now there are several thousand. This growth has been spurred on by aggressive marketing using sport celebrities and social influencers in advertising, as well as the promotion and acceptance of sneakers as fashionable and comfortable for general use outside of sport. It can be said that sport is an industry firmly on the ground but flying high.

Notes

l. 01 **cross trainer**「クロストレーニングシューズ」あらゆる運動に適したスポーツシューズ
l. 01 **cleats**「(滑り止め具のついた) クリート靴」
l. 02 **traction** = the ability to hold the ground without sliding
l. 07 **closure**「(空いているところを) 閉じる道具」
l. 07 **lace**「(靴などの) 紐」
l. 08 **Velcro**「ベルクロ」米国ベルクロ社の商標で面ファスナーの一種．日本では，マジックテープとも呼ばれている．
l. 10 **elasticity**「弾力性；伸縮性」(e.g. This rubber band has lost its elasticity.)
l. 17 **molecule**「分子」
l. 22 **tread**「靴底の紋様」
l. 22 **ridge**「(細長い) 隆起部」
l. 22 **groove**「溝」
l. 37 **pronation**「回内 (運動)」
l. 37 **supination**「回外 (運動)」
l. 53 **spur on**「拍車を掛ける」
l. 54 **celebrity**「有名人；著名人」単に名前が知られているだけではなく，マスコミを通じて大衆の関心を集める人を指す．

Warm-up Exercise

39

A 下記の写真を見たのち、1-3 の質問文と選択肢を聴いて正しい答えを選びなさい。

1. What kind of sport shoes are they wearing?
   (A) (B) (C)
2. What are they doing?
   (A) (B) (C)
3. How many players are wearing uniforms with odd numbers?
   (A) (B) (C)

Inspiration Exercise

B 次の 1-3 の英文を聴いて下線部を補い、さらにその意味を表している本文中の語を答えなさい。

1. This is the ________________________________ of a shoe.
   In other words: (   )
2. This means to be ________________________________.
   In other words: (   )
3. This is an adverb which means ________________________________
   ____________________.
   In other words: (   )

Word-attack Exercise

C 次の (1) ～ (3) の本文中に出現している語（下記対象語が複数出現していても、ここでは本文中に網掛けしてある語）と最も近い意味で使用されている英文を (A)(B)(C) の中から選びなさい。

1. material
   (A) Let's listen to Madonna's 1984 track *Material Girl* on Apple Music again.
   (B) The florist arranged the flowers, some of which were made out of plastic materials.
   (C) We felt relieved to know that the statements by the president are free from material error.
2. appearance
   (A) The politician made a brief appearance towards the end of the farewell party held for the musician.
   (B) The appearance of organic vegetables in the supermarkets has completely changed the eating habits of the people living in the area.
   (C) It was rumored that Anne was the kind of woman who takes too much pride in her appearance.
3. absorb
   (A) One of the famous companies in Japan has finally been absorbed into a foreign-affiliated company.
   (B) The whole audience was listening to this music with absorbed interest.
   (C) My husband was so absorbed in watching the baseball game on TV that he didn't hear the door open.

Comprehension Exercise

D 本文の内容に即して、次の英文の内容が正しければ T (True) を、誤っていれば F (False) を記しなさい。

(　　) 1. Most footwear manufacturers say that the most important elements in selecting footwear materials are cushioning and support.

(　　) 2. “Elasticity” refers to how well a material maintains its shape and size after wearing it for a long time.

(　　) 3. An athletic shoe is designed to have a flexible sole, suitable tread and the ability to absorb impact.

(　　) 4. When choosing a running shoe, you have to know your own running style.

(　　) 5. The RS-Computer shoe model contains a miniature computer in order to collect exercise data during athletic performance.

Discourse Exercise

E 次の出だしに続く英文を意味の通るように並べかえなさい。

The materials used in sport footwear are determined based on their functions and the market.

A. An athletic shoe needs to have a flexible sole as it absorbs force during different motions.

B. Then, aggressive marketing is applied in order to spur growth in the sport footwear industry.

C. As well as that elasticity requirement, stability and density influence the type of material used for sport footwear.

Answers. (　　　　) ☞ (　　　　) ☞ (　　　　)

Production Exercise

F 下記の英文の問いに対する理由のひとつとなるように (　　) 内の語を並べ替えて正しい英文にしなさい。

Why is it so important to wear the right shoes for running?

Because a quality shoe (damage / can / you / prevent / ankle / and / foot / help / to).

Ans. Because a quality shoe ....

Unit 14

Adventure is for Fashion!

【変化し始めたアドベンチャーの流儀】

Although there have always been individual women travelers who brave the outdoors in order to experience adventures in nature, until recently the majority of adventure travelers have been male. The reasons for this are varied, but mainly they were due to social and cultural restrictions: fears over safety, roles of women that promoted home life and duties, religious attitudes, limited female access to money, beliefs that exercise and sport were largely male pursuits, and so on. In the past, athletic equipment and clothing have been typically designed with the male body in mind, resulting in frustration and lack of comfort for women with an interest in outdoor recreation and travel. However, sociocultural attitudes towards female participation in outdoor adventure activities changed dramatically in the 20th and 21st centuries.

Perhaps because of the rising number of females in the workforce as well as the decrease in average family size in more developed countries, the current global trend is toward more financial security and independence for women. As a result, they may have more disposable incomes than in the past for leisure activities such as shopping, dining out, and travel. The fashion industry, with sales commonly much greater for women than for men, has recognized this phenomenon and has been aggressively designing and promoting adventure recreation fashion for women. People who have blogs to self-promote and show off their personal lifestyles and fashion choices (so-called “influencers”) can be followed by many others on the Internet, and a fashion company often improves its sales when a popular influencer is wearing its apparel.

In Japan one such online style icon is Yuri Yosumi. She started trekking in 2003 and began blogging with photos of her own style of trekking clothes, focusing on the pleasures of getting out in nature and dressing attractively at the same time. Her mountain outfits include colorful tights or leggings paired with shorts or skirts, both comfortable and fashionable. Such posts about mountain fashion and exercise quickly popularized trekking among women in Japan, Taiwan and Hong Kong. Soon, so many groups of fashion-conscious women took up trekking that they were given the nickname “Yama Girls” (Mountain Girls).

What distinguishes Yama Girls from male trekkers is not only their great interest in outfits but their behavior during hikes. Whereas men are usually relatively quiet and often hike in small groups, Yama Girls are often large, talkative female-only groups who spend their treks chatting and complimenting each other about their clothing, particularly those who live in urban areas where shopping is a popular pastime.

The new importance of female adventure recreation is apparent in many ways. Unlike in the past, modern mountain huts frequently have private rooms and flush toilets in order to make them more attractive to women. More and more adventure travel companies are providing group tours exclusively for women, not only for trekking but for a variety of other outdoor adventures such as white-water rafting, canyoning, and horseback trekking. For these tours the main criteria are adequate fitness, enthusiasm, and a love of nature. Adventure Women, a US-based travel company offering worldwide tours, notes "Most of our guests are traveling solo, some for the first time. But many also enjoy sharing their adventure vacations with friends, mothers, daughters, partners, and/or sisters."

It is apparent that the trend towards female adventure travel has been encouraged by a combination of factors such as increased wealth, fewer family duties, better accommodation choices, and improved clothing fashions. Moreover, women are aware that through such adventure recreation they can meet new people, challenge themselves by learning a new skill or activity, be physically active, and enjoy an independent break from family or work.

Notes

l. 15 **disposable income**「可処分所得」
l. 19 **show off**「見せびらかす」
l. 20 **influencer**「社会に対して大きな影響を与える人；情報発信者」
l. 22 **apparel** = clothing ; dress
l. 26 **outfit**「（特定の目的のための）服装ひとそろい」（e.g. I need to get some outfits for my business trip.）
l. 31 **distinguish ~ from ...**「～を…と区別する；～を…と見分ける」
l. 32 **whereas**「それに対して；ところが」
l. 36 **pastime**「娯楽；気晴らし」（e.g. Golf is my favorite pastime.）
l. 42 **white water** = water in a river that flows quickly and has a lot of bubbles
l. 42 **canyoning** = canyoneering（米）
l. 43 **criteria**「（判断・評価などのための）規準；尺度」（sing.）criterion

Warm-up Exercise

42

A 下記の写真を見たのち、1-3の質問文と選択肢を聴いて正しい答えを選びなさい。

1. Where are they walking?
   (A)　(B)　(C)
2. What kind of sporting equipment are they using?
   (A)　(B)　(C)
3. Why are the two women probably leaning towards each other?
   (A)　(B)　(C)

Inspiration Exercise

43

B 次の 1-3 の英文を聴いて下線部を補い、さらにその意味を表している本文中の語を答えなさい。

1. This is a person ________________________________ and is thought to represent an important idea.
   In other words: (   )

2. It is the sport of traveling ________________________________ by means of a flat, floating structure.
   In other words: (   )

3. The word means a result or product in which ________________________________ ____________________.
   In other words: (   )

Word-attack Exercise

C 次の (1) ～ (3) の本文中に出現している語（下記対象語が複数出現していても、ここでは本文中に網掛けしてある語）と最も近い意味で使用されている英文を (A)(B)(C) の中から選びなさい。

1. current
   (A) It is dangerous to swim at the mouth of the river because the current is so strong.
   (B) Your current driver's license works as acceptable ID in the country.
   (C) We can start this brand-new car with alternating current.

2. post
   (A) One of my friends will post her comment about the incident on her Twitter soon.
   (B) My father resigned the post of president of the company.
   (C) People in our country need to come to terms with the post-covid world.

3. break
   (A) If students break the rules, they will be punished.
   (B) He is the last man to break his promise.
   (C) After finishing school, I really need a break from studying.

Comprehension Exercise

D 本文の内容に即して、次の英文の内容が昔の女性に関するものには P (Past) を、現代の女性に関するものには N (Now) を記しなさい。

( ) 1. Women have less disposable income.
( ) 2. Women have fewer family duties.
( ) 3. Women go to the mountains wearing fancy clothes.
( ) 4. Women are busy with housework.
( ) 5. Women believe that sports and exercise are mainly a male interest.

Discourse Exercise

E 次の出だしに続く英文を意味の通るように並べかえなさい。

In the past most adventure travelers were men, while female participation in those adventures was almost unheard of.

A. This trend led to the social phenomenon of apparel companies trying to increase the production of adventure recreation fashion to support women's outdoor activities and travel.

B. Those women went out for work, gaining more independence as well as more disposable incomes for the pursuit of their personal interests.

C. However, in the 20th century more and more women started to become freer from their home duties.

Answers. ( ) ☞ ( ) ☞ ( )

Production Exercise

F 下記の英文は、無料のウェブ翻訳ツールで和文入力して訳出したものであるが、語用的誤用が生じて不自然となっている。本文の英語表現を参考に、下線部についてよりわかりやすい表現にかえなさい。

【入力和文】

「山ガール」を大まかに解釈するなら、それは自由な時間に野外活動を楽しんでいる若い都会暮らしの女性ということになる。

【訳出文】

* The rough interpretation of "Mountain Girl" is that it is a young urban woman who enjoys doing outdoor activities in her free time.

Ans. ……………………………………………………

…………………………… who enjoys doing outdoor activities in her free time.

Unit 15

Esports

【e スポーツのジレンマ】

Video games, with us for several decades, were first developed by computer scientists in the 1950s for their own research and entertainment. By the 1970s, video gaming had gained enough interest that video arcades sprouted up in many places. Furthermore, new video tools such as joysticks and home gaming consoles allowed people to play video games on their home TVs. Later, the invention of liquid crystal display (LCD) for TV and computer screens—a technology that enabled much sharper images—made gaming easier on the eyes when playing. From the 1980s onwards, gaming computers, online gaming, and handheld LCD games were all the rage. Eventually so many people, particularly in Asia but ultimately everywhere, were playing video games online or together with friends in arcades or at home that a new leisure category of competitive gaming named "esports" was born.

Although it was originally just a fun leisure pastime for amateurs within the video game culture, competitive gaming with leagues and tournaments has now become a serious professional field. It was the availability of live streaming technology around the world that made esports an important part of the video game industry. Realizing its potential for huge audiences and rich profits, commercial businesses are now sponsoring elite individuals and teams in professional esport competitions. Many game developers are actively designing new software and games as well as funding esport events in order to promote sales and increase the fan base.

Esport video games fall into a number of types, with MOBA (multiplayer online battle arena), FPS (first-person shooter), card games, and RTS (real-time strategy) being some of the most-known genres. Esport events are steadily gaining fans and participants because video games can now be played or watched in both private and public settings. Moreover, unlike in traditional sports like swimming or volleyball, it is not necessary to be in top physical condition to play an esport. In fact, it is because of this lack of necessity for athletic fitness that some people have argued that esport is not really a sport at all.

Then, how can we define a 'sport'? Is something a sport merely because it is labelled that on television? The Oxford Advanced Learner's Dictionary calls sport an "activity that you do for pleasure and that needs physical effort or skill, usually done in a special area and according to fixed rules." From that definition, activities like hunting, fishing, darts, or poker might not truly be sports—even though they are usually called that. However, another way of thinking about sport is that it is an activity that requires training, fast reflexes, dexterity (hand-eye coordination), mental concentration, and game knowledge. Within the esport world at least, it is axiomatic (unquestionable) that esport is in reality a sport. As a consequence, the esport industry has been pressuring the IOC (International Olympic Committee) to include it in the 2024 Paris

Olympics.

However, the IOC has so far only agreed for esports to be considered as a non-medal competitive event at some future Olympics. The IOC says that the violent content of many video games is contrary to the peaceful spirit of Olympic competition, so only esports that simulate traditional sports will ever be accepted as an Olympic sport. Furthermore, the IOC recommends that video games which require physical actions by the player (using virtual or augmented reality, such as by literally making a "batting" motion with a handheld game console when playing virtual baseball) are more likely to be accepted as legitimate Olympic sports in the future.

Regardless of the opinions of the IOC or other sport organizations, esports is already a major economic industry with strong media exposure, supported by at least 2.3 billion players and fans worldwide. As an example of this, "The International 2019," an esport tournament with 18 sponsored teams and 90 professional players had a prize pool of more than $34 million raised entirely by crowdfunding (through online funding campaigns). Esport is clearly a roaring lion!

Notes

l. 03 **video arcade**「ゲームセンター」
l. 03 **sprout up**「急成長する」
l. 04 **joystick**「（ビデオゲームの）操作レバー」
l. 09 **handheld**「携帯（型）；手で持って操作できる」
l. 09 **all the rage**「大流行している；ブレイクしている」
l. 15 **live streaming**「ライブ・ストリーミング」ライブの音声や動画を，ストリーミングでダウンロードしながら再生すること．
l. 21 **fan base**「ファン層」
l. 36 **fast reflexes**「素早い反射神経」
l. 37 **dexterity**「器用さ；機敏さ」（adj. dexterous）
l. 38 **axiomatic**「公理の；自明の」（n. axiom）
l. 47 **augment** = increase
l. 55 **prize pool**「賞金総額」
l. 56 **roaring lion**「うなり声をあげているライオン」

Warm-up Exercise

A 下記の写真を見たのち、1-3 の質問文と選択肢を聴いて正しい答えを選びなさい。

1. What are they playing with?
   (A) (B) (C)
2. What are they wearing on their heads?
   (A) (B) (C)
3. What are they doing?
   (A) (B) (C)

Inspiration Exercise

46

B 次の 1-3 の英文を聴いて下線部を補い、さらにその意味を表している本文中の語を答えなさい。

1. This is a handle you use ________________________________
   on the computer screen.
   In other words: (   )

2. This word means any hobby or activity ________________________________
   ________________.
   In other words: (   )

3. This is the ability ________________________________ you are doing.
   In other words: (   )

Word-attack Exercise

C 次の (1) ～ (3) の本文中に出現している語（下記対象語が複数出現していても、ここでは本文中に網掛けしてある語）と最も近い意味で使用されている英文を (A)(B)(C) の中から選びなさい。

1. console
   (A) We don't know how to console him for the loss of his daughter.
   (B) I tried to console her with her favorite music, but in vain.
   (C) None of my friends knew how to use the console in my room.

2. label
   (A) All of the newspapers without exception labelled the TV commentator a troublemaker.
   (B) The British rock group switched to a new label last year and recently released a first album.
   (C) I'm afraid the label which shows the expiration date of the medicine has come off.

3. consequence
   (A) The young singer was interviewed by the music magazine as a woman of power and consequence.
   (B) The lack of effective medication may have disastrous consequences for the public health of the country.
   (C) It is of little consequence whether the earthquake took place early in the morning or late at night.

Comprehension Exercise

D 本文の内容に即して、次の英文の内容が正しければ T (True) を、誤っていれば F (False) を記しなさい。

( ) 1. The number of professional players of esports is increasing.
( ) 2. It is necessary for the players to be physically strong to play esports.
( ) 3. Esports doesn't fall into the category of "sports" if a "sport" is defined by training, concentration, and game knowledge.
( ) 4. The IOC currently accepts esports only as possible non-medal events due to their frequent violent contents.
( ) 5. Esports might become legitimate Olympic sports in the future as long as they require significant physical actions by players.

Discourse Exercise

E 次の出だしに続く英文を意味の通るように並べかえなさい。

As competitive gaming continued to evolve from the 1980s onwards, esports gradually became a new leisure category in online gaming.

A. One reason for its popularity is that taking part in an esport competition does not require athletic fitness.

B. So esports have become a major economic industry with extensive media coverage.

C. Furthermore, live streaming technology allowed esports to be shared with a wide online audience.

Answers. ( ) ☞ ( ) ☞ ( )

Production Exercise

F 次の和文に対する英訳が完成するように ( ) 内に適する語を入れなさい。

この大学の e スポーツビジネスオンライン修士課程は、拡大する e スポーツの分野で成功するために必要な理論的かつ実践的教育を提供します。

The online master's degree in esports business at this university ( ) students ( ) the ( ) and ( ) education ( ) ( ) ( ) in the expanding field of esports.

執筆者

浅間正通　梅田 泰　Egitim Soyhan　大石敏也　小川あい　古西美佐子
Joey LeDrew　Nicholas Lambert　西村厚子　山下 巖

執筆協力者

Mariam Ala-Rashi　林 順子

ALIVE AND ACTIVE　[B-951]
健“幸”ライフ志向の総合英語

1　刷　2023年2月7日

編著者　浅間　正通　Masamichi Asama
ニコラス・ランバート　Nicholas Lambert
山下　巖　Iwao Yamashita

発行者　南雲一範　Kazunori Nagumo
発行所　株式会社　南雲堂
〒162-0801　東京都新宿区山吹町361
NAN'UN-DO Co., Ltd.
361 Yamabuki-cho, Shinjuku-ku, Tokyo 162-0801, Japan
振替口座：00160-0-46863
TEL: 03-3268-2311（営業部：学校関係）
03-3268-2384（営業部：書店関係）
03-3268-2387（編集部）
FAX: 03-3269-2486

編集者　加藤　敦
表　紙　Nスタジオ
組　版　Office haru
検　印　省　略
コード　ISBN978-4-523-17951-1　C0082

Printed in Japan

E-mail　nanundo@post.email.ne.jp
URL　https://www.nanun-do.co.jp/